T0315187

"Mallory Erickson wants us all to succeed. She has taken on that mission with an approach that is both vulnerably personal and pragmatically empirical. She leads by example, sharing her own emotional struggles and uncovering sometimes-uncomfortable truths in a profession that can be uniquely challenging.

In this book, Erickson dismantles common fundraising myths and misconceptions that so often lead to counter-productive practices. Recognizing that fundraiser behavior is the primary influencer of donor action or inaction, she provides science-backed, practical advice that leads to better outcomes.

What the Fundraising is a clear guide for an industry in dire need of new approaches. It is a thoughtful and caring manual that moves fundraisers from struggling to thriving. This book is for every fundraiser who feels isolated and uncertain and for every nonprofit leader looking for a direct way to be accountable for their own success."

—Woodrow Rosenbaum
Chief Data Officer of Giving Tuesday

"Mallory Erickson's *What the Fundraising* sheds crucial light on the often overlooked causes of burnout in the nonprofit sector. By illuminating the brain-body connection, she empowers fundraisers to understand and address the underlying stressors. This book is a groundbreaking resource for sustainable success in social justice and beyond."

—Dr. Linnea Passaler
Author of Heal Your Nervous System

"Erickson has penned an essential read for anyone seeking to make a significant contribution to the nonprofit sector. *What the Fundraising* combines strategic insights with heartfelt advice, providing a roadmap for fundraisers to navigate their sacred roles with confidence and an alignment-first approach that is incredibly effective, ultimately reshaping the way we think about and approach fundraising."

—**Natalie Rekstad**
Founder & CEO of Black Fox Global

"We live in a world where scarcity mindset is lived and celebrated in different forms. A constant lingering sense of fear and competition feels like the starting point for almost every task. Our sector (nonprofit) is no different when it comes to fundraising. The scarcity mindset – that we lose if someone else wins or, if I center myself, my energy, I will be left behind in our arbitrary timelines – that affects how we show up in this work (and our success measures). All of it affects our behaviors, expectations, and intentions to the point that it convinces us to clutch tightly to what we have, fearing loss more than we crave meaningful, collaborative growth.

I am so grateful Mallory's book exists in this world now – enabling every reader to work on that relentless fear. This book allows us to see possibilities and approach trust-building in a completely different way. I appreciate the thoughtfulness and thoroughness in every chapter – that repeats the very important message – that abundance mindset is a practice of joy and purpose. The blended life coach and data scientist in me can't wait to pick up this book a few times a year."

—**Meena Das**
CEO of Namaste Data

"*What the Fundraising* shows the power of shifting mindsets and applying new frameworks to daily life. Mallory's application of the concepts in *Energy Leadership* to the fundraising field empowers fundraisers to reach new heights. Her compassion, tenacity, and belief in her colleagues' potential have created a masterful playbook, destined to be a go-to resource for years to come."

—Bruce Schneider
Author of Energy Leadership and Founder of the Institute for Professional Excellence in Coaching (iPEC)

"In *What the Fundraising*, Mallory Erickson leads the charge on the future of fundraising with unparalleled insight and empathy. As someone deeply entrenched in the nonprofit sector, I can attest to the chronic challenges fundraisers face daily—stress, burnout, and a relentless chase for donations. Erickson's groundbreaking work shifts the paradigm from a transactional, dollar-driven approach to one of alignment, empathy, and sustainable impact.

Fundraisers are exhausted because we've been conditioned to focus solely on donations rather than co-building an aligned DREAM with our donors. Mallory's book eloquently transforms this mindset, offering a revolutionary approach that fosters genuine connections and shared goals.

This book is not just a guide; it's a manifesto for lasting change. By addressing the root causes of stress and burnout in the sector, Erickson paves the way for a healthier, more vibrant nonprofit community.

What the Fundraising is an essential resource for any nonprofit professional, especially those on the front lines of fundraising. This book challenges fundraisers to improve their well-being, effectiveness, and results by adopting a comprehensive, people-focused approach. Mallory Erickson's innovative insights pave the way for a more promising and impactful future in fundraising, turning it from a stressful endeavor into a powerful force for enduring, significant change. It is essential reading for anyone committed to driving meaningful progress in the world."

—**Floyd Jones**
Founder of BackBlack

"Mallory breaks down what can be seen as an incredibly scary and overwhelming process of fundraising into very practical and embodied steps that help your body and nervous system feel safe to raise money in an aligned and authentic way. What a gift this book is for fundraisers."

—**Ruthie Lindsey**
Author of There I Am

"*What the Fundraising* by Mallory Erickson is a hilarious and brutally honest guide to the sometimes chaotic world of nonprofit fundraising. Erickson doesn't just pull back the curtain; she rips it off the rod and sets it on fire. This book is a must-read for anyone who's ever felt like raising money is like juggling flaming torches while riding a unicycle on a tightrope—blindfolded.

As a Black woman with 25+ years experience as a development professional and trusted philanthropic advisor, I can confidently say I wish I had this book when I was at my lowest. Erickson's insights are a lifeline for those navigating the nonprofit sector's labyrinth of underfunding, lack of trust, and unrealistic expectations. She tackles the unique challenges I faced with a blend of empathy and wit, making it clear that fundraising is less about the money and more about surviving the circus.

If you've ever wondered why your brilliant ideas are met with skepticism or why your funding proposals seem to vanish into a black hole, *What the Fundraising* will resonate deeply. Erickson's blend of personal anecdotes, research-backed themes and strategic advice is both empowering and laugh-out-loud funny. She captures the essence of what it means to be a fundraiser in this field today: resilient, resourceful, and ready to turn every obstacle into an opportunity for growth.

In short, *What the Fundraising* is the ultimate survival guide for anyone brave enough to tackle the nonprofit sector. It's not just a book; it's a revolution wrapped in humor and hard truths. Get ready to laugh, cry, and most importantly, thrive."

—Kishshana Palmer
Author of Busy Is a Four Letter Word:
A Guide to Achieving More by Doing Less

"Don't let the word "fundraising" mislead you. This book is for anyone who creates, holds, and manages relationships – meaning everyone. For impact leaders and changemakers who are looking to navigate the world in a new way, this book is a guide to follow. According to the National Science Foundation, 80% of our thoughts are negative and 95% of our thoughts are repetitive. Mallory's ability to address and dismantle the common negative self-talk in order to thrive and hold healthy relationships is refreshing and inviting. Her vulnerable and practical approach to business and the nonprofit sector is a robust and sustainable new model that we all need to adopt and integrate into our daily lives; instead of remaining worn-out, unmotivated and stressed.

Mallory's unique Powers Partners Formula™ teaches fundraisers how to raise more from the right funders by combining the best science-backed practices in fundraising strategy, executive coaching, habit and behavior design, and design thinking. In addition, this book shares executive coaching tools and insightful research provided by psychologists and scientists – combined, these elements form a comprehensive foundation to proactively address and resolve many challenges that funders and relationships managers encounter.

What the Fundraising is an essential resource for professionals, especially those in fundraising roles, who want to feel better, do better, and raise more, finally overcoming the challenges they face in their drive to catalyze lasting change in the world. A book to add to your quiver if you want to thrive in today's world!"

—Whitney Clapper
Community Relations and
Impact Lead at Patagonia

WHAT
THE
FUNDRAISING

WHAT THE

THE

FUNDRAISING

Embracing and Enabling the
People Behind the Purpose

MALLORY ERICKSON

WILEY

Published by John Wiley & Sons, Inc., Hoboken, New Jersey.

Published simultaneously in Canada.

For general information on our other products and services or for technical support, please contact our Customer Care Department within the United States at (800) 762-2974, outside the United States at (317) 572-3993 or fax (317) 572-4002.

Wiley also publishes its books in a variety of electronic formats. Some content that appears in print may not be available in electronic formats. For more information about Wiley products, visit our web site at www.wiley.com.

Library of Congress Cataloging-in-Publication Data is Available:

ISBN 9781394213856 (cloth)
ISBN 9781394213900 (ePub)
ISBN 9781394213917 (ePDF)

Cover Design: Wiley
Cover Image: © tortoon/Getty Images
Author Photo: © Jin Han

SKY10081511_081424

For Emmie and Ila: May you grow up in a world surrounded by generosity and a thriving nonprofit sector.

For fundraisers: May you always know how sacred and important your work is.

Never forget your worth, and remember to prioritize your well-being—you matter.

Contents

Introduction

Like so many fundraisers, I became one accidentally.

A few years out of college, I applied for jobs in the nonprofit sector and got hired for a position to run a community garden. Though I didn't know anything about plants, I was eager to get my hands dirty, so to speak. Soon after starting in a program director role, I found myself doing almost anything the organization needed, including hiring, event planning, curriculum design, and student trip management. Wearing multiple hats is not an uncommon experience for people working in the nonprofit sector.

As the years went by, promotions followed. I zigzagged through my organization's hierarchy, and even though I was responsible for developing programs and had little to do with fundraising, I was catapulted upward to managing director of the entire organization. With that title came a silent but pressing responsibility—raising money. Lots of money. Money I didn't know how to ask for.

As the first person in the organization to step into this role, there was no onboarding process, little guidance on how to perform the daily tasks required, and definitely no advice on managing the intense emotions from being ghosted or rejected when asking for thousands of dollars. And forget about any tips for how to ask for that amount of money in the first place. My boss sent me out with a few home-printed brochures, a mission statement, and a vague directive to raise money by just "building relationships."

Here's the truth: I didn't have the slightest clue about how to become a successful fundraiser. It wasn't like I was an accountant who trained to be an accountant. I was a political science and sociology major with a master's in education and a garden job that I was learning on the fly. And so, I scrambled. At the time, I didn't know of any class or Nonprofit 101 training that could ease my anxiety, and it seemed like everything was on the line: my salary, my community garden, and the future of other planned garden projects for which I had unintentionally become responsible. I didn't know where to start, but I knew I wanted to make a difference in the world and that it took money to have the impact I wanted to have.

So, I decided to just try "this fundraising thing" with no clue what I was getting into.

Making the Ask

I remember my first "big ask." My boss arranged for me to meet a key donor at a coffee shop. I got to the spot a little bit early to change in their bathroom from my dirt-caked Carhartt overalls into a pencil skirt. After this quick change, I returned to my car, so nervous I honestly felt like I was going to throw up. (This lesson would come much later, but the shift from running the environmental literacy program to fundraising needed more than just a change of clothes.) As I sat in my front seat reviewing notes, a hummingbird zipped by and snacked from a feeder in front of the cafe. I straightened out my clearance-sale skirt and felt my heart rate match the pace of the hummingbird's wings.

Just an hour before, I had been present and authentic in the garden with my students, connecting with the kids and feeling alive. If you had asked me then, with my hands in the soil, I could have passionately articulated the importance of our environmental education programs and the urgent need for them in schools nationwide.

But as I sat in my car and tried to prepare for the donor meeting, my sense of purpose and confidence were gone. My palms were clenched and pulsing at my sides. I grabbed the meeting briefing sheet from my backpack and read through the donor's previous involvement with our organization and their large past donations. It was extensive. Even as I prepared to meet with someone who clearly believed in our organization, I felt like I was going into this meeting to ask someone to do something they really didn't want to do: donate.

This thought—that I was trying to strong-arm someone into giving—created a toxic power dynamic in my head. The thought then developed into a narrative that I believed was true: the donor had the money and thus all the value, while I had nothing to offer them. This story solidified my inferior position. I (the fundraiser) was trying to get the person with more power (the donor) to give me something I didn't deserve.

Sweaty palms, a racing heart, and nausea ensued as I tried to settle my nerves and reconcile my smallness to my big ask. "Breathe, Mallory," I heard myself say. "Think positive." But even though my brain tried to counter these worries with practiced abundance mantras, it was useless. To my core, I felt unworthy. My body was trapped in the tension of the unspoken power dynamic and uncertainty.

It didn't help that I had been told to "build a relationship" with the donor before discussing money. That felt so confusing—how do I build a genuine relationship if I feel like I can't be completely transparent or feel like I have a hidden agenda? How do I build a strong relationship if I'm too frightened to speak freely? What do I pretend the relationship is about if it's not ultimately about investment in my organization?

Two minutes to our meeting time.

I took one last deep breath, opened the car door, and stepped out into the spring sunshine. As I walked toward the coffee shop, layers of my true self fell away. When I got to the door, I was a performer, a shell of who I really was.

As I entered the air conditioning, I had a fleeting moment of recognition that this was no way to build real relationships. All other real relationships in my life were based on trust and transparency—so why would this be any different? But I shoved that thought away and pulled my shoulders back. This version of fundraising—persuading, hounding, begging, trying to be selected as worthy—was all I knew.

As I rounded the corner to find the donor's table, I gave myself one final pep talk. "Make it work, Mallory. Get the money." Even though I ultimately raised money during the meeting, I felt so much discomfort in my body that I was sure I was a terrible fundraiser because of it.

What the Fundraising

The thought "Will I ever be good at this?" stayed with me for years. It popped up every time I met with a donor, and the answer was clear by the time I walked out: no. But I kept trying even when I switched organizations and found myself yet again responsible for raising money.

Even in a new environment, the negative self-talk, downward spiraling, and endless pressure never subsided. My days dragged: meeting with a donor, writing marketing materials, sending emails, asking for donations, and getting ghosted only to be thrust into another donor meeting. I managed. I cried. I kept going, trying to make a difference. As soon as I realized that fundraising meant holding the organization's fate in my hands, I never felt more alone.

After some time, things took a turn for the worse. I started to get sick. Really sick. My job made me physically ill. After a few years of this desperate, plea-focused event and campaign hamster wheel, strange aches started to wind down my spine from all the tension, resulting in pain that became chronic. Sleepless nights and bedridden days followed. Thoughts raced through my mind: there's no way good fundraisers feel like this. I must be a bad fundraiser.

My pain, I would realize years later, was deeply tied to how I was taught to fundraise: the pressure to appear like I had it all together, to accept money from anyone, to treat money as the only thing of value, and to give in to the power dynamics that were intrinsically tied to the nonprofit system as a result of transactional fundraising methodologies. My chronic stress was also tied to my perfectionism, my tendency to please others, and my habitual self-criticism. This was compounded by feelings of unworthiness in my role as a fundraiser and the constant uncertainty I felt about reaching that forever-moving fundraising benchmark on which the fate of my organization rested.

My body was physically suffering due to the ongoing stress and negative thinking. The situation deteriorated to the point where I nearly quit the nonprofit sector. At the lowest point in my career, I made a pivotal discovery. I initially thought my brain and body were working against me, but they were actually acting as the alarm I needed to make a change. I chose to stay and explore new approaches to fundraising.

Since those early years in the trenches of frontline fundraising, I have gone from exhausted and miserable to empowered, embodied, and legitimately enjoying this work. How? I learned ways to manage my discomfort and shift my fundraising practices so I could raise more for my organization sustainably and reliably. What once felt impossible—fundraising without chronic stress and overwhelm—became my reality once I understood and honored a new methodology of fundraising focused on alignment.

My unique framework—the Power Partners Formula™—teaches fundraisers how to raise more from the right funders without hounding people for money. Since its inception in 2021, I have trained more than 60,000 fundraisers using elements of this win-win framework, which combines the best science-backed practices in fundraising strategy, executive coaching, habit and behavior design, and design thinking.

In this book, we won't cover every tool in the formula, but we will explore some core elements that shape my approach: modern fundraising strategy, executive coaching tools, and insightful research provided by psychologists and scientists on my podcast, *What the Fundraising*. Together, these elements form a comprehensive foundation to preemptively address and resolve many of the challenges fundraisers encounter.

Central to this exploration is the integration of executive coaching tools. Executive coaching enhances performance, develops leadership skills, and fosters personal growth. It offers a process of self-discovery that enhances our consciousness of our beliefs and behaviors, and reveals internal barriers to our success. This methodology is particularly valuable in a field like fundraising, where self-awareness, emotional intelligence, and a deep understanding of human behavior are essential.

I've spent the last five years learning about systemic negative emotions in the nonprofit sector and exploring how those emotions can be mitigated, managed, and improved by executive coaching tools. These tools enable us to see where our beliefs, emotions, thoughts, and actions intersect with our results. Executive coaching teaches us how to harness our power, redirect our own thoughts, break negative beliefs, and create actions that empower us to achieve our goals.

What's interesting about executive coaching is that the tools map with what psychologists and neuroscientists have noticed about the human autonomic nervous system, which contains two systems: the sympathetic nervous system and the parasympathetic nervous system. In this book, we are going to focus on the sympathetic nervous system, which is the internal alarm clock and defense system that all mammals have to protect against threats and danger.

You might not be familiar with the term *sympathetic nervous system*, but you are likely familiar with the terms our culture uses to describe it: *fight or flight*. This phrase, coined by physiologist and Harvard medical professor Walter Bradford Cannon (1871–1945), describes the unconscious biological reaction mammals experience when encountering a threat (Cannon 1915, 211). If our body chooses to fight when in the sympathetic nervous system, it can result in anger, fists, and raised voices. The flight response, although it might literally propel someone to run away, primarily manifests in modern society as procrastination, avoidance of difficult conversations, intellectualization, overworking on unrelated tasks, and excessive preparation.

Although fight or flight dominated the conversation for most of the 20th century, researchers have recently identified several tertiary responses, one of which is freeze. Studies have shown that when mammals experience a threatening situation, central neural pathways activate, causing the body to literally freeze. We often experience this "freeze response" when we experience intense fear. We might not all drop to the floor, but a freeze response can manifest as withdrawal, emotional numbing, paralysis in decision-making, or complete disengagement.

Other nuanced experiences can occur, yet fighting, fleeing, and freezing are some of our primary methods of dealing with conflict, fear, and threats. No matter which response our bodies choose, it signals a stress response. A stress response is complex, but it often emerges as physical symptoms like goosebumps, nausea, the urge to scream (fight), the desire to run away (flight), or feeling paralyzed and unable to act (freeze).

But why does this matter for fundraisers?

In my research, I have found that traditional fundraising experiences like ghosting, power dynamics, and isolation, as well as emotions regularly experienced by fundraisers, like overwhelm, self-doubt, guilt, unworthiness, and fear of rejection, are linked to episodes of fight, flight, and freeze, resulting in the chronic stress that leads to burnout.

When we experience chronic stress or burnout, the consequences are severe. In addition to the impact on our mental and physical health (which should be enough right there!), science has shown that humans who experience chronic stress also biologically struggle to build authentic relationships and connect with other humans (Dana 2018). Chronic stress also prevents decision-making, limits empathy, and prevents people from engaging in the community, all of which are necessary to do our jobs.

Although I am not a neuroscientist or psychologist, I've interviewed top psychology and neuroscience experts on my podcast *What the Fundraising* to discover the largely unrecognized connection between the nervous system and the enablement and success of fundraisers. The experience and emotions psychologists and neuroscientists use to describe chronic stress closely correlate to the Energy Level Index® assessment provided by iPEC, the Institute for Professional Excellence in Coaching, where I received my coaching certification. But no matter which framework you explore—executive coaching or psychology—the results are clear: when humans experience chronic stress, we cannot make decisions or connections, and we definitely can't fundraise effectively.

Through my research and coaching, I've realized that people are expecting the linchpin of the third largest employment sector in the United States (fundraisers) to do our work in a state of near-constant panic, stress, and overwhelm, which is the exact psychological state that inhibits our ability to take the actions most critical to fundraising: building relationships. Our psychological state is increasingly important to understand when we consider how stress further affects our behavior.

In 2023, I surveyed fundraisers about how they felt about their jobs, and when asked what they do when they feel stressed about asking for money, 75% of fundraisers stated they do a task that's not fundraising. So, not only does stress affect our ability to build relationships but it also hinders our ability to take any fundraising action at all.

This means that fundraisers who are experiencing chronic stress will fundamentally struggle to perform the tasks every webinar, consultant, and online course tells them is the key to fundraising successfully: creating engagement opportunities and building authentic relationships. Stressed-out fundraisers, thus, cannot fundraise in efficient and effective ways. All of this matters because we depend on fundraisers to support the fundamental existence, never mind growth, of the nonprofit sector.

Although the fight, flight, and freeze responses are subconscious experiences, with the knowledge of their existence, we can prevent these biological systems from dominating our reality. Instead of being activated by situations that cause stress, like a big donor meeting or an important pitch presentation, we can tap into executive coaching techniques that help manage our stress response during these activities so that we can remain authentic, embodied, and open to connection.

Fundraisers need to be able to take effective action and authentically connect because relationships and engagement inspire donor behavior. Most training and conversations focus on fundraising actions as if they are an easy task list and the subsequent donor outcomes are simple if-then statements. For example, if I just pick up the phone

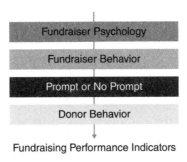

Figure I.1 Donor behavior is a response.

and call the donor, then the donor will increase their donation. If I send a mass text message, then we will reach our campaign goal. Those things might be true, but when we oversimplify, we're missing one of the largest influencers of success—how the fundraiser feels while taking those actions. Donor actions are primarily reactions to the way fundraising is conducted and serve as lagging indicators in fundraising data. This is why the experience of fundraisers is so important—because the effectiveness of fundraising is closely linked to the stress levels of the fundraisers themselves. Higher stress can hinder fundraisers' ability to establish relationships or to prompt donors, making it less likely for donors to engage and participate. This is why we need to focus on the fundraisers before we can focus on the fundraising. At the end of the day, fundraiser behavior is the leading indicator of fundraising success (Figure I.1).

Who You Are and Why We're Here

If you are reading this book, you care about the state of the nonprofit sector. You are firmly aware that giving is down across the sector, and if the sector continues to decline at this rate, the nonprofit sector will ultimately disappear. According to a report from the Fundraising Effectiveness Project, there have been decreases in the number of donors (of all giving sizes, but especially among individual donors giving small gifts between $1 to $100), the number of dollars given, and the rate of donor retention (particularly for the largest donors)

(Fundraising Effectiveness Project 2023). This stark reality has massive implications for society.

In 2019, Giving USA reported the lowest giving level in 40 years (Gamboa 2023). To underscore the dip, research from the Indiana University Lilly Family School of Philanthropy noted that in 2000, an estimated 66% of Americans gave to charity. By 2014, this figure decreased to 55%, and in 2016, it fell to 53%. Currently, that number has dipped to less than half of Americans (Indiana University Lilly Family School of Philanthropy 2023).

Nonprofit value, expertise, and commitment are needed everywhere: in education, where the nonprofit provides additional classes and services to children; to health care access, where we launch and fund clinics and doctors in areas with inadequate medical access; to the environment, where organizations research and implement strategies to reduce climate change. No matter the location, mission, or receiving benefactors, nonprofits are critical to the planet's and humanity's success. Moreover, the nonprofit sector serves as the bridge between society and government. Where the government doesn't provide much needed social services, we step in.

Beyond the services and programs that nonprofits provide, the nonprofit sector is the third largest in the United States, employing 11.9 million people—only retail trade and manufacturing out-mass nonprofits in employment (Salamon 2018). The decline of the sector will have layers of impact on society.

There aren't enough conversations happening about how important the nonprofit sector is to our economy and society, but even fewer conversations are happening about the folks who bring in all the money to make the work possible: our fundraisers.

Fundraisers

Fundraisers, by definition, are responsible for moving money into the sector. Yet many who "do fundraising" don't identify as a "fundraiser." The truth is, I didn't call myself a fundraiser for many years. That term felt uncomfortable and full of stigma. I didn't want any of that, and yet I was still doing the work. I put in long hours and devoted years of my life to the mission. I was deeply committed. Yet, like so many of us, I was very uncomfortable doing my job's basic duties, like asking for money, dealing with rejection, and receiving large sums of money.

If you are one of these people, I want you to know that you're not alone, and you are not a "bad fundraiser" because you feel uncomfortable or overwhelmed by your responsibilities. I wish I could go back in time and tell my younger self that most fundraisers deal with discomfort and resistance in one way or another. It's normal. And it doesn't mean anything is wrong with you.

In fact, it makes perfect sense that doubting yourself, getting rejected, and getting ghosted would stress you out. It's how the human body works. Again, we, and all other mammals, have a nervous system that is more than 500 million years old, and it's trained to keep us safe. Asking for money is uncomfortable for most people, and so it's activating our natural biology to run away from the threat. But, although it might feel like it when it comes to the level of stress in your body, that donor isn't a lion trying to eat you. I want to assure you that there are ways to approach fundraising without constant fear, doubt, or being on the brink of tears. It's possible to engage in this work feeling calm, secure, and empowered.

When we have the right tools, when we learn to honor the deep relationship between our mind and body, and move resources in alignment and toward our values, fundraising can be an energizing, sacred, and healing act. Fundraising can change once we can internalize that, calm our system, and learn how to step into our true inherent power.

Sector Leaders

If you aren't a fundraiser and find yourself here, you might be someone fundraisers rely on. Perhaps you are a sector leader: a nonprofit consultant, a leader at a tech company that supports nonprofits, a community member, a donor, the head of the foundation, a board member, or maybe a corporate philanthropist. I want to invite you into this conversation and urge you to stick around when it feels uncomfortable.

You play an important role in this dialogue, but you might not be aware of some of the limitations frontline fundraisers face. There is a problem with the state of fundraising, and it actually goes much deeper than lack of money, donors, or even time. The root of the problem originates with how the sector thinks about fundraisers. This knowledge gap is hurting your primary goal: moving more money into the nonprofit sector and fulfilling the missions and visions of the organizations you support.

In addition to what we cover in this book, sector leadership needs to start to prioritize key performance indicators that enable fundraisers to break out of transactional methods and prioritize the actions that lead to healthy fundraising practices, sustainable donor engagement, connected relationships, and fundraisers who actually want to stay in their roles. As I often say, don't tell me what you care about, show me what you track. I hope this book provides additional clarity on why this shift is so critical.

The First Step Forward

The future of the nonprofit sector depends on providing fundraisers with tools that support the whole fundraiser—including the inner experience of the fundraiser—not just templates or trainings that focus solely on fundraising strategy. It's crucial to create a path forward.

This book is my contribution to that effort. It's designed for anyone committed to a more equitable and just world, recognizing that this goal is intrinsically linked to the well-being of nonprofits. And the well-being of nonprofits is directly connected to the health and wellness of the people inside of them. Viewing the health of the sector through this perspective means caring about global issues while also caring about individual fundraisers and our ability to connect and build strong relationships. If we lose this capacity, the entire nonprofit sector risks collapse.

Alignment Fundraising

Once we learn the tools of executive coaching and use those tools to harness our energy and ground our system, we will be able to increase how present we are in our fundraising work. We will be able to build truly authentic relationships with donors that honor the value fundraisers and organizations bring to the table. This shift will enable us to move away from hounding people for money and start to identify mutually beneficial strategic partnerships.

There is a strategy and process to this: it is the methodology I call ***Alignment Fundraising***. Alignment Fundraising gives us the opportunity to transition from a scarcity mindset and self-doubt, and is rooted in the idea that great fundraising is not an ask; it's an offer. However, for us to implement Alignment Fundraising in our organizations, we have to be connected and aligned within ourselves. By addressing our own limiting beliefs and inner barriers, we prevent much of the chronic stress, overwhelm, and fear that describes the experience of so many fundraisers. Instead, we get to build Power Partnerships. Working with Power Partners makes fundraising more sustainable and feels good to all involved. This is a wildly different approach than what we typically see in this sector.

What Is Possible with Alignment Fundraising

Once I created and applied the principles of Alignment Fundraising, I led the transformation of an organization's revenue from $1 million to more than $3 million in a short time and with relative ease.

But the most significant change was that I began to enjoy fundraising. I felt more present, empowered, and connected. Alignment Fundraising helped me realize I could engage with funders differently, inviting them to partner with me instead of just soliciting donations. This approach shifted the power dynamics, creating a relationship of equality rather than neediness. I stopped merely asking for money and started offering people the chance to contribute to something meaningful. This change in perspective led me to seek out Power Partners instead of just donors.

With this mindset shift, I could finally go to funder meetings calmly and ask, "Do we have the same goals and values?" If the answer was yes— *great*. We could move forward to talk about what might be possible if we decided to work together. If it was a no, it was no problem. It wasn't about me, and the no gave me the clarity to move on and prioritize my time efficiently.

Over the last few years, I've helped more than 300 organizations find their Power Partners. The framework empowers them to overcome limiting beliefs, feel confident in their fundraising methods, build long-term relationships with funders, and successfully raise more money.

What the Fundraising teaches elements of this framework while giving sector leaders a unique insight into fundraisers' daily lives and struggles.

Inside *What the Fundraising*

Chapter 1 explores how we've reached the current critical tipping point in the sector. We'll take a closer look at the history of philanthropy and how its foundations of tax incentives and racism still affects today's philanthropic landscape. We'll also look at the decline in giving and the staffing crisis in our sector and how the two correlate.

Chapter 2 gets right to the issue of scarcity mindset and how this mindset leads to transactional fundraising. We'll discuss the fundraising norms that make it harder to do our jobs and create problems with our funders, and we'll start to think about how to move beyond transactional methodologies.

Chapter 3 reminds us of why fundraising sometimes feels cringy. We address the stigmas about our jobs and our internal dialogue that makes things more difficult. We also dive deep into the toxic underbelly of the ways our work burns us out and how these pressures can compound into serious chronic issues by exploring the nervous system's way of communicating with us. We bring it full circle by explaining how this nervous system activation and chronic stress inhibit our ability to build relationships and connect with donors, essentially sabotaging good fundraising.

Chapter 4 begins our reprieve from sector-caused burnout and stress. We'll dive into executive coaching tools outlined in *Energy Leadership: The 7 Level Framework for Mastery in Life and Business* by Bruce D. Schneider, and the Energy Leadership® Index assessment provided by iPEC (n.d.), which give us a framework to make more sustainable and beneficial choices. We learn more about how we make decisions and the inner blocks such as limiting beliefs, assumptions, and interpretations, which often hold us back. Once we can understand how our energy level affects our work, we'll start to learn how to validate, acknowledge, and reframe negative or spiraling thoughts into curiosity and clarity.

Chapter 5 introduces the Alignment Fundraising method. We'll apply our new understanding of our energy levels and executive coaching tools to different funding opportunities. We'll explore the motivations of individual, corporate, and foundation funders and learn to develop strategic, mutually beneficial, and aligned partnerships that last. We'll also start mapping assets to help us see the value in our organizations, as well as how to attract and retain aligned partnerships.

Chapter 6 demonstrates how to build connected and authentic relationships through the application of the research compiled in *What the Fundraising*. We're going beyond the platitudes of "just building relationships" and diving into what makes a strong partnership, how to earn and retain our partner's trust, and why we should continue to prioritize alignment above all else. We also have some helpful tips for some of the most vulnerable fundraising moments such as dealing with rejection and talking about overhead.

The **Conclusion** considers the deeper questions about the emotional and systemic challenges in fundraising, proposes what's next, and shares gratitude for the work we continue to do.

Acknowledging Underlying Systemic Issues

The nonprofit sector faces many underlying systemic issues, including racism, classism, and sexism. These deeply embedded forces have shaped the history and present reality of our sector. Nonprofits that work with and center disproportionately affected communities, including communities of color, LGBTQ+, and disabled communities, have faced extraordinary challenges securing necessary funding. Nonprofit workers whose identities are marginalized in our sector routinely face extreme opposition, including structural barriers that make fundraising work particularly difficult.

I wrote this book to make accessible the tools that I have found helpful in my own journey as a fundraiser, but I am under no illusion they will fix the systemic inequities that shape our sector. White supremacy, sexism, and ableism determine the context in which we do our fundraising. I am grateful to the sector leaders whose work is helping us unpack and more deeply understand these intersecting issues. I particularly want to acknowledge the work and thought leadership provided by the Community Centric Fundraising community and books such as *Emergent Strategy: Shaping Change, Changing Worlds*, by Adrienne Maree Brown; *The Revolution Will Not Be Funded: Beyond the Non-Profit Industrial Complex*, edited by INCITE!; and *Collecting Courage: Joy, Pain, Freedom, Love—Anti-Black Racism in the Charitable Sector*, edited by Nneka Allen, Camila Vital Nunes Pereira, and Nicole Salmon, and featuring contributions from Nneka Allen, Camila Vital Nunes Pereira, Nicole O. Salmon, Olumide (Mide) Akerewusi, Naimah Bilal, Birgit Smith Burton, Christal M. Cherry, Nicole E. Cozier, Sherrie James, Fatou Jammeh, Muthoni Kariuki, Heba Mahmoud, Niambi Martin-John, Kishshana Palmer, and Marva Wisdom. These thought leaders and resources, among many others, have advanced this critical analysis and the necessary solutions for our sector.

In this book, I will present strategies and solutions for what I believe to be many of the reasons we experience exacerbated chronic stress as fundraisers. They are generalizations and do not account for the complexity of fundraiser identities, trauma, workplace toxicity, neurodivergence, or any other layer and lens through which we do this work. This is not because these experiences don't matter, but because they matter immensely and deserve focused attention from those with expertise and lived experience. My hope is that the tools shared here inspire inquiry, challenge, adaptation, and further development that can continue to strengthen our collective work to create change and improve our organizations.

Case Studies and Research

Throughout this book, I feature Power Partners Formula™ clients. We explore their individual relationships with fundraising, chronic stress, and the steps they took to positively affect their well-being and improve their fundraising.

We also explore research from top neuroscientists, psychologists, fundraising experts, and thought leaders—pulled mostly from interviews I've hosted on my podcast *What the Fundraising*. For a full list of episodes, topics, and links to the guest's work, visit malloryerickson.com/allshows. Through candid conversations, we explore the nervous system, our human ability to connect, and how chronic stress inhibits our ability to reach our goals.

I will connect the dots between the research and interviews with fundraisers to showcase the correlation between our stress and nervous system and our ability to succeed. My goal with these case studies and research is to paint a picture I've clearly seen in my life and work: there is a relationship between how our brains and bodies work, and our ability as fundraisers to move money into the sector.

Finally, I refer to my own experiences as a fundraiser and then as an executive coach to further demonstrate the correlation between fundraisers' success and our ability to stay in calm, connected states. I use personal anecdotes to showcase what I've noticed to be true about the relationship between what is happening inside of us and our ability to fundraise and the profound shift I've seen in those who use Alignment Fundraising. When I made this shift and learned to pay attention to my chronic stress and more consistently stay in a connected state of mind, I could raise millions of dollars with more ease and less stress.

But I also want to make something clear: my research is incomplete. Our work as fundraisers and the landscape we navigate is always changing. So, there may be something that won't carry over after this book is published. I am not done learning and growing just because I've chosen to publish this book. Not only do I recognize that a lot of the scientific research references are limited in their Western-centric lens and stem from white-normative culture, but I also know I haven't learned everything out there about the challenges that different fundraisers face. I always allow grace and space to stay curious, stand corrected, or change my mind as my research, perspective, and opinions evolve. I invite disagreement and conversation to unfold from this analysis and from that, I know we will push the conversation and this sector forward.

Whether you are a sector leader or a fundraiser, here is what I want you to know: there is a different, better, and more sustainable future possible for our sector. When we take what we know about being human and apply it to our work, opportunities expand. I hope this book will provide a transformative shift in how we address the challenges in fundraising and the current giving crisis. It is imperative that we start by redirecting our attention toward understanding, supporting, and improving the lives of fundraisers.

It is time we finally, truly, embrace and enable the people behind the purpose.

PART
I

The Problem

1

A Critical Tipping Point

2020 brought the world to a screeching halt. The nonprofit institutions I had worked for and loved my entire career closed right before my eyes. The COVID-19 pandemic brought unprecedented levels of fear, paralysis, and anxiety. Despite the tremendous need for nonprofit services, the sector was contracting with layoffs happening at record speed, sending the workforce home to wait. Nonprofit staff members and those who benefited from their services were suffering.

With after-school programs closed, addiction programs stopped in mid-track, and most in-person activity halted, the nonprofit sector was unable to operate at its previous capacity. I felt like all I could do was watch helplessly, reading updates from my networks and seeing reports scroll across my screens. As the world shut down and efforts shifted to support emergency responders, medical teams, and at-risk populations, any unrelated giving was initially set aside. Nonprofits mirrored the rest of the world, halting fundraising efforts for their own causes—even though they were losing tremendous amounts of money. Nonprofits seemed to feel it was inappropriate to ask for money for their work amid an uncertain global crisis.

Yet, with everyone sheltered at home and without the distractions and priorities of normal life, another type of generosity emerged: people tapped into their creativity, posting concerts, virtual meet-ups, and free educational courses—anything to try to help. Despite the suffering, we saw a surge of hope, inspiration, reflection, and desire to serve. So, I asked myself, "What can I do right now? How can I support those in the nonprofit sector?"

During our time home, I was wrapping up my iPEC Executive Coaching Certification and had just read Bruce D. Schneider's *Energy Leadership: The 7 Level Framework for Mastery in Life and Business*. With the new knowledge and tools to work through fear and anxiety, I developed ways to share this information with my fundraising colleagues and network. I felt strongly that we should not stop fundraising because it could lead to long-term detrimental consequences for the communities we serve.

I started by offering a free group coaching call focused on fundraising resistance and fears. I wanted to help fundraisers take action, even if they held limiting beliefs that doing so was inappropriate. I typed up a Google Form, posted it in a free fundraising Facebook group, and went to sleep.

The next day, 180 people had signed up. The form wasn't even connected to a website. I didn't have a presentation put together. I remember walking away from my husband, who was bouncing our eight-month-old baby girl on his lap, and saying, "Oh my gosh." I knew the sector needed help strategizing how to move forward while operating with limited resources, but I did not expect such a resounding "yes!" to my invitation.

Over the next few days, I pulled my Fearless Fundraising curriculum together, focusing on developing a resource to support our sector and create a lasting, positive impact. However, my tools and strategies were a little out-of-the-box compared to other fundraising consultants and coaches. I knew introducing ideas from Schneider's *Energy Leadership* such as energy levels and limiting beliefs and applying them to fundraising might take some people way outside of their comfort zones, but I experienced the benefits myself and understood how powerful these frameworks could be.

The message and tools resonated. I taught more than 1,000 people in 2020, launching my coaching career. Connecting with fundraisers helped me gain deeper insight into the nonprofit sector's challenges and the current giving crisis. Listening to stories from fundraisers across the country opened my eyes to the broader dynamics of giving, funder behavior, and fundraisers' experiences and put a spotlight on the systemic racism and misogyny entwined with the nonprofit sector. I had the opportunity to dig deeper to discover more about the sharp decline in giving trends over the past decade, and to work with experts in our field to seek solutions.

The National Council of Nonprofits surveyed nonprofit leaders and found that 7 out of 10 nonprofits (70.5%) anticipated charitable donations to decrease or remain flat in 2023. About the same number (68.7%) expected the number of donors to decrease or stay flat (National Council of Nonprofits 2023). Their anticipation of decline is not unwarranted. The survey cited a report to underscore these pessimistic views: "Last year [2022], charitable giving by corporations, foundations, and individuals, and bequests to support the work of nonprofits decreased by 3.4% in current dollars and 10.5% adjusted for inflation, according to the latest annual Giving USA report."

That decline has a huge impact: the American nonprofit sector alone employs nearly 12 million people. Within that ecosystem are roughly 1.8 million US-based 501(c)(3) organizations, including public charities, private foundations, and other organizations (Faulk et al. 2021). Together, nonprofits serve a wide range of communities across the United States, with many focusing on the most vulnerable populations, historically marginalized, and low-income communities. A report by the Urban Institute found that 45% of national nonprofits focus programming on communities below the federal poverty level. Most of these organizations rely on traditional fundraising methods—based on foundations, trusts, and individual giving—to support their causes (Faulk et al. 2021).

Nonprofits are facing hardships from both ends: fewer funds are coming in and more staff members are burning out and leaving the profession. As the sector experienced an intense decline in giving over the past several years, fundraisers have left their jobs in droves. A *Chronicle of Philanthropy* survey from 2019 found 51% of the fundraisers surveyed (in the United States and Canada) expected to leave their jobs within the next two years; most worryingly, about 30% said they would leave the fundraising field altogether in the next two years (Joslyn 2019). This was a concerning statistic before the pandemic put additional stress on nonprofits.

If organizations continue to contract, it's difficult to imagine what will happen to our sector and those who rely on the benefits of our fundraising efforts. This starts with fundraisers on the ground. If organizations are barely staying afloat, what resources are available for fundraisers themselves? If huge portions of the workforce are leaving due to burnout and lack of support from leaders, who will bring money in to support our essential work?

The pandemic did not create these issues within the nonprofit sector; it only brought them into the spotlight in a different way. If we take a closer look at some of the history of nonprofits, a clearer picture begins to form.

Giving in the Gilded Age

The Gilded Age in the United States (1865 to 1904) represented a 40-year period of economic growth, industrialization, and the explosion of the number of wealthy elites. In the 1870s, there were about 100 millionaires in the United States. By 1892, the *New York Tribune* reported 4,047 millionaires. By 1916 that number ballooned to nearly 40,000 (Curti et al. 1963). Many of these millionaires became wealthy through extreme exploitation of land, resources, and people.

The same technological and managerial developments that led to a boom in industrial fortunes required cheap labor to staff the factories, build the railroads, and grow the economy. Workers streamed into booming cities and mill towns from rural areas across the United States. Immigration spiked as the demand for cheap industrial labor continued to grow. In the rapidly expanding cities, workers experienced horrendous social conditions, including intractable poverty, dangerous and exploitative labor conditions, and unmanaged public health crises.

During this wildly unequal and rapidly transforming world, modern philanthropy was born.

George Peabody (1795–1869), the partner and patriarch behind the legendary banking company J. P. Morgan, is considered the father of modern philanthropy (Bernstein and Swan 2008). Born to a low-income family in Massachusetts, Peabody clawed his way up through the financial sector and accumulated one of the world's largest personal fortunes. In 1867, he used this wealth to establish the Peabody Fund, whose mission was to strengthen education for newly freed enslaved people in the South. The Peabody Fund was incorporated as a foundation, which was (and still is) the preferred economic model that enables wealthy people to consolidate their money with relative tax advantages. This model created a system where the foundations controlled and distributed funds to various benevolent and reform associations (the ancestors of our modern nonprofits), religious and educational institutions, and favored causes (The George Peabody Library n.d.).

Philanthropy in the Gilded Age was further shaped by the influence of Andrew Carnegie and his essay "The Gospel of Wealth" (Carnegie 1889). Carnegie's steel fortune positioned him as one of the richest men in modern history, who spent the second half of his life theorizing and practicing philanthropic giving. He believed wealthy elites had an obligation to improve society through philanthropic giving under the leadership of the elites themselves, rather than through tax-funded government programs. He advocated to "help those who will help themselves" and to avoid supporting "the slothful, the drunken, the unworthy," contributing to the normalization of harmful stereotyping of less fortunate and marginalized communities. This mindset and attitude cast a shadow over philanthropic work and propagated the idea that only certain individuals were worthy of assistance. Carnegie focused his giving on education, libraries, and other social causes that aligned with his political and moral beliefs about deserving and undeserving recipients.

The first trust was established in 1907 by Margaret Olivia Slocum Sage, who inherited a fortune from her husband, railroad baron Russell Sage (Russell Sage Foundation n.d.). Sage's fortune was built, among other things, on the backbreaking labor of Chinese railroad workers who endured inhumane and exploitative conditions while constructing the Union Pacific transcontinental railroad (Gandhi 2021). When her husband died and left her an estimated $63 million, Margaret turned her attention to philanthropy. She aligned with many of Carnegie's ideals from "The Gospel of Wealth" and wrote her own 1905 treatise, "Opportunities and Responsibilities of Leisured Women" (Sage 1905). Sage argued that women such as herself should be "helping the unfortunate by providing them with a good environment, opportunity for self-support and individual responsibility, and protection from the unscrupulous." Like Carnegie, Sage had strict ideas about who and what was deserving of philanthropic support and argued that wealthy women had a particular role to play in guiding social reform. Her investments in early health care, city planning, religious causes, and teacher training programs were heralded as exemplary uses of industrial wealth. The Russell Sage Foundation is still active today and focuses on social science research (Russell Sage Foundation n.d.).

Following the examples of Carnegie, Peabody, Sage, and others, foundations and trusts became fashionable and savvy ways for elites to consolidate, control, and distribute large amounts of money without having to pay taxes—a strategy still used today.

Although tax, foundation, and trust law have shifted and changed over the last 100 years, the model of philanthropy established in the Gilded Age has remained. We have inherited a system where (in most cases) the donors with the dollars maintain decision-making power, and their priorities and values are pursued over and above those of the recipients and staff in the philanthropic sector.

Taxes and Nonprofits

The Revenue Act of 1913 established the modern federal income tax system and 501(c)(3) tax-exempt status. While taxes increased, organizations that served "the public good, as opposed to private interests" qualified for tax exemptions. Specifically, "organizations that are exempt under IRS section 501(c)(3) are those whose purposes are religious, charitable, scientific, literary, or educational" (Arnsberger et al. 2008, 110). For the first time, individuals could deduct from their personal taxes any contributions made to a tax-exempt organization, which incentivized donations to newly christened 501(c)(3) s.

The Revenue Act of 1917 further aimed to boost philanthropy at a time when income tax rates escalated to fund World War I. The following year, charitable bequests became eligible for deductions, and by 1936, corporations were also allowed to claim charitable deductions. These developments, together with the high wages and taxes of World War II and its prosperous aftermath, later set the stage for the nonprofit boom in the second half of the 20th century.

The Tax Reform Act of 1969 finally crystallized the definition of a private foundation under the national tax code. This act established fundamental dos and don'ts for private foundations, including standardized reporting, a ban on lobbying, and a 5% annual minimum distribution amount, ultimately legitimizing the private foundation as a giving vehicle. The dramatic increase in private foundations, from 22,000 in 1980 to more than 86,000 by 2017, underscored the persistence of a model that continues to put wealthy donors at the center of the work (Steuerle and Soskis 2020). This multibillion-dollar philanthropic ecosystem emphasizes the need to fulfill donor preferences and requirements, often even at the expense of the needs and well-being of beneficiaries.

During the neoliberal era, spanning from the 1970s to the present, tax laws continued to evolve, further solidifying the tax-deductible model of philanthropy. This period was marked by a significant rollback in state welfare provisions and led to an ideological shift where the responsibility for social welfare increasingly fell on the private sector, particularly nonprofit organizations. This shift was heavily influenced by right-wing policies that advocated for increasing privatization, individual responsibility, and reducing government spending on social services—all resulting in a vacuum that nonprofits were called on to fill. "At the same time that the government scaled back social services, it deployed expensive systems of incarceration and penal welfare," effectively making it more difficult for vulnerable individuals to seek help after being incarcerated (Britton-Purdey et al. 2021). In Massachusetts, this looked like "state refined systems of parole and child support to make poor people, disproportionately of color, 'get to work or go to jail'" (Britton-Purdey et al. 2021). These policies and their Carnegie-esque assumptions of worthy and unworthy recipients of assistance were mirrored across the United States, relying on harsh policing and a cold justice system instead of investments in equitable opportunities for rehabilitation and access to education or job training.

Meanwhile, the tax-deductible model of philanthropy became a crucial mechanism through which wealthy donors could freely give to their chosen causes—and strategically shield their profits from taxation. Carnegie's philosophy in "The Gospel of Wealth," where the wealthy directly led and funded philanthropic efforts, echoed in the 20th century as tax incentives that encouraged elites to play a more prominent role in social welfare. However, unlike Carnegie's vision, the neoliberal model often involved channeling funds through nonprofits—effectively passing off the responsibility of addressing social issues to these organizations, while allowing private citizens to retain discretionary power and control over their funds.

Neoliberalism marked a sea change in philanthropy, one that not only changed the landscape of social welfare provision but also altered the dynamics of wealth distribution and social responsibility. As philanthropy in this era shifted away from the collective responsibility for social welfare, nonprofits became a crucial voice in addressing social inequalities—albeit often working within the constraints and limitations set by their reliance on private funding and the framework of the tax-deductible donations.

Systemic Inequities: Then and Now

There is no discussing the history of philanthropy in the United States without addressing its deeply problematic legacy of wealth, race, and privilege. From its roots in the Gilded Age through to modern neoliberalism, the priorities of the nonprofit sector have traditionally been dictated by affluent white individuals, typically without any input from the communities they seek to support. Too often, leaders of color in this sector find themselves pushing back against the weight of this legacy, which casts them and their communities as problems to be solved rather than leaders to support and learn from.

Private foundations, many of which represent generational wealth passed down across decades, give more than a billion dollars a year, but very few of these dollars reach the communities who need them most—especially those that were originally exploited to generate the wealth in the first place. According to Edgar Villanueva, author of *Decolonizing Wealth: Indigenous Wisdom to Heal Divides and Restore Balance,* "Only about 7.5% to 8% of grants from foundations in the United States go to communities of color. And less than 1% goes to Native American communities" (Villanueva 2021). The disparity is particularly stark when seen in a comparison between similar groups: Echoing Green, an early-stage funder for nonprofits, found that organizations focused on improving the outcomes of Black boys with Black leaders had 45% less revenue and 91% less unrestricted assets than their counterparts with white leaders (Echoing Green 2020). Even philanthropic leadership itself doesn't look much different than it did a century ago: 92% of foundation leaders and 80% of foundation staff are white (Shea 2016).

In response to these inequities, many leaders like Michelle Shireen Muri, cofounder of the Community-Centric Fundraising movement and founder of Freedom Conspiracy, are in deep discussion about the impacts of colonialism, whiteness, and the systematic ways that people of color are prevented from gaining access to generational wealth. A key takeaway from Muri's work is the urgent need to reconceptualize how nonprofits operate. The sector's reliance on traditional forms of philanthropy, rooted in paternalistic approaches and perpetuating systemic inequalities, calls for a critical reassessment.

Muri also emphasized the power dynamics within nonprofits, highlighting how development directors can influence narratives and shape organizational policies. She argues that the traits often seen as positive in nonprofit culture, such as perfectionism and aversion to conflict, may in fact be manifestations of white supremacy culture:

> I believe that some of the currents of resignation from typically optimistic and energetic people are actually characteristics of white supremacy culture. Primary among them is our tendency to chase perfectionism, the fear that making one mistake could actually be confused with being a mistake. White supremacy culture tells us that being honest and transparent—by voicing our mistake, a tension, or a conflict—could mean punishment or banishment. White supremacy culture teaches us to be overly cautious and "inoffensive," and that has us spending time and energy trying to make sure that people's feelings aren't getting hurt by the truths that we secretly want to share. Fear of open conflict suppresses us. Defensiveness suppresses us. Thinking in the binary doesn't help us, because there are often more than two options! Solutions and problem-solving aren't either/or. When we look at things in a binary way, we may lose sight of complexity and, more importantly, humanity . . . [characteristics] of white supremacy culture do not serve our community. And when we know better, we must do better, and that means that we must take it upon ourselves to recognize that we are powerful, and we must wield our power to interrupt the dynamics that disempower us and keep us from doing our best work for our organizations! (Muri 2020)

As Muri further pointed out when she joined me on my *What the Fundraising* podcast, taking a community-centric approach involves recognizing the systemic issues that prevent organizations from effectively addressing societal problems. Her words call for a shift in power dynamics. "This is about having power with other people, not power over other people" (Muri 2023).

But as we try to address power imbalances, we cannot ignore that industries have thrived on the existence of inequity, with the non-profit sector itself being a product of these systemic disparities. In Villanueva's (2021) *Decolonizing Wealth*, he reminds us philanthropy was designed to preserve the wealth and privilege of a few by maintaining systemic inequities. This perpetuation of inequity not only ensures we fail to address the root causes of the disparities but also sustains the very gaps philanthropy claims to be trying to close.

Whatever the noble intentions of nonprofit work, the sector was set up in such a way that the pursuit of social good intersects with financial strategies to protect wealth created through exploitation. Racism and exploitation helped mold modern philanthropy and created the nonprofit industrial complex as we know it today, and that very history still holds the sector back. In addition to highlighting the problems the sector is facing now, this historical context sheds light on the experience of fundraisers of color today.

In environmental conservation work specifically, "despite the value of BIPOC-led work in this field, the InDEEP researchers found white-led organizations are more resourced and better funded than BIPOC-led organizations. An analysis of data from Candid for the five-year period from 2014 through 2018 found the funding gap between white-led and BIPOC-led environmental and conservation organizations is approximately $2.7 billion. In that five-year period, a total of $3.7 billion was awarded in the environmental and conservation field, with $3.2 billion going to white-led organizations and $498 million going to BIPOC-led organizations" (InDEEP Initiative n.d.).

"Overcoming the Racial Bias in Philanthropic Funding" published in *Stanford Social Innovation Review*, gives an account of what leads to this gap. The article tells the story of an Alaska Native–led nonprofit organization up for a grant renewal at the same time as an organization led by one of his white peers (Dorsey et al. 2020). The white CEO secured funding in three months while it took the CEO Mike Roberts, who is an enrolled member of the Tlingit tribe, 18 months to secure funding. This is despite the fact that Roberts's organization had been receiving grants from the foundation for 25 years.

In the story, Roberts reflected on the differing dynamics he faced compared to his white counterpart, namely that he was under more scrutiny and needed to provide more justifications, finding "himself having to defend his organization's approach and its demonstrated success." Roberts said, "That kind of privilege, that access, that trust— it's pretty powerful, and awful. And that disparity is just what happened to us recently. I have similar stories for nearly every grant we go for" (Dorsey et al. 2020).

This imbalance underscores the ingrained biases within the philanthropic world, which is further complicated by the inherent power dynamics in funder relationships. When we permit or fail to challenge patronizing narratives that surround leaders of color, we continue to let feel-good stories overshadow factual complexities and neglect the voices and agency of the communities involved. We also perpetuate the discrimination and lack of support that fundraisers of color continue to experience within their own organizations. Christal M. Cherry, one of the contributors of *Collecting Courage: Joy, Pain, Freedom, Love—Anti-Black Racism in the Charitable Sector*, a collection of true stories documenting racism and survival by 15 accomplished Black fundraisers working in charities across North America, said, "I wanted to share about my personal journey as a fundraiser. I had been fired a few times, but being let go wasn't the worst part. The pain, humiliation, and attacks on my character and self-esteem were the most piercing. Fundraising is about treating others with kindness and thoughtfulness in order to build trusting relationships. It's about being gentle with our donors. Fundraising is innately human, yet in my opinion I wasn't treated humanely" (Cherry n.d.).

When it comes to fundraising and nonprofit leadership today, Muri reminds us, "Just because [something is] working doesn't mean it's right. Just because whatever fundraising method we're using is really effective in raising money, for example, does not mean that it's ethical" (Muri 2023).

I would argue that not only is it not ethical but it isn't working either.

The Decline in Giving

Philanthropy today is at a turning point. At the beginning of the 21st century, two-thirds of American households gave to a philanthropic cause (Indiana University Lilly Family School of Philanthropy 2024). Cut to today, less than half of households donate to charity. The total number of Americans who donate has significantly decreased, while high-net-worth individuals dominate the donor space. In truth, if it weren't for MacKenzie Scott, who has given away more than $16.5 billion between 2019 and the time of this publication, America's philanthropic impact would have significantly decreased over the last three years (Safronova 2021). In short, overall giving has grown, but fewer people are participating (Edworthy et al. 2022). We are once again in a situation where the priorities of only the very wealthiest Americans dominate the space.

The Fundraising Effectiveness Project (FEP) was established in 2006 to inform the nonprofit sector on key trends in giving. The FEP quarterly report covering the period from January to September of 2023 shows declines in the number of donors, the number of dollars, and the rate of donor retention. Some of the largest declines were among small donors—donors giving under $100 declined by 16% and donors giving between $101 and $500 declined by 8% (Fundraising Effectiveness Project 2023). These downward trends carry significant implications for the nonprofit sector because small donors represent

84% of all giving. Coupled with the decline in new donors, down 22% from the previous year, these statistics help to explain why we have seen a weakening in the total number of dollars donated. The FEP 2023 report serves as a cautionary signal, highlighting such patterns in giving and urging nonprofits to address these challenges proactively.

There has been a lot of analysis put forth about the primary reasons for the decline in giving to nonprofits. There are many pieces to the puzzle, but none of the existing arguments give us the full picture of the dynamics we're seeing in the sector. Some of the most commonly cited factors include broad cultural patterns like trends in religious affiliations, changes in the economy, changes in tax codes, and the decline in trust and purpose in nonprofits. During the past several decades, there have been notable declines in adults expressing an affiliation with religion. In 2020, less than half of US adults reported belonging to a church, synagogue, or mosque, a significant drop from the 70% of Americans who attended religious services in 1999 (Jones 2021). This is important for nonprofit giving because those who associate with a religion are more likely to give to charity (both secular and nonsecular), and to give in the largest amounts (Giving USA 2017).

The continuous decline of the average American's spending power also has an impact on their ability to give. The Great Recession resulted in a 7% drop in giving in 2008 and an additional 6% in 2009, and the sector did not recover for at least five years. During and following the COVID-19 pandemic, health care nonprofits saw increases in donations, while many other nonprofits saw declines in revenue upward of 50% (Sinclair 2023). As the world adjusted to the pandemic's challenges, giving across the sector took a hit, slowing substantially (Fundraising Effectiveness Project 2023).

When we factor in the financial difficulties of the average household and the impact of the steep rise in inflation since 2019, we can see how trust in the government, and trust in others trickled down to adversely affect people's ability to trust in nonprofits (Pew Research Center 2023). Although most Americans continue to trust nonprofits, generally speaking, there are notable trends by generation. Although

67% of baby boomers reported trust in nonprofits, only 46% of Gen Z adults expressed a sense of trust (Morning Consult 2022).

Some people blame the decline on recent changes to tax law, but I don't think that explains the whole picture. The Tax Cuts and Jobs Act of 2017 and other tax law changes initially raised concerns about reduced incentives for charitable giving; however, the actual impact on overall charitable contributions has been less straightforward. The data indicates that individual giving continued to rise despite changes in the tax code, suggesting that factors other than tax incentives, such as personal motivations, play a significant role in charitable giving. This doesn't imply we should completely ignore these changes, or any of the challenges cited, because they all affect people's ability and incentives to give to nonprofits. But my argument asserts that we will see bigger changes in the sector if we have the capacity to tap into the motivations and personal identity of all donors to incentivize giving beyond simple variables like tax codes. There's a lot on our plates, but we can't ignore the fact that when there are meaningful engagement opportunities for donors, their contributions are higher (Ramchandani 2023).

It seems we are being asked to do more with less on all fronts—lack of funds is affecting staff sizes; workloads demand our goals and funds raised reach pre-pandemic levels despite the lack of support from the organization; donors might have less to give, yet increasingly seek personalized experiences and direct connections with the causes they support. When we consider these factors all together, also remembering that fundraisers are feeling the same impacts while still showing up and inviting people to contribute, we don't need to wonder why our colleagues are burned out and discouraged.

The Staffing Crisis

Nearly 3 out of 4 nonprofits (74.6%) that completed the National Council of Nonprofits survey reported job vacancies, more than half of nonprofits (51.7%) reported they have more vacancies now compared to before the pandemic, and nearly 3 out of 10 (28.1%) have longer wait lists for services (National Council of Nonprofits 2023).

Beyond the business cost of hiring, training, and then sending fundraisers out into the community, the overturn of employees hurts nonprofits in other ways. As mentioned by Candid, a nonprofit dedicated to gathering data and informing the social sector, high turnover in fundraising positions "compromises the precious commodity of trust donors place in the nonprofit. No donor likes constantly being introduced to a stream of new staff who have yet to learn their stories, personalities, and likes and dislikes" (Eskin 2021). The results tell us that when their relationships with fundraisers are severed, roughly 25% of donors make smaller gifts, delay their contributions, or stop giving altogether. This issue extends beyond fundraisers struggling to build relationships between the organization and the donor; it highlights how revolving doors create a pervasive sense of instability and disconnection.

They Aren't Separate Problems

If we are looking at a persistent decline in giving, and we see there is a paralleled chronic decline in retention for those doing the asking, doesn't it make sense to correlate the two? It's two sides of the same coin: asking for and giving money to nonprofits (in the way we have historically) isn't working for most of the people involved anymore.

The philanthropy model we have inherited from history, which prioritizes the interests and values of wealthy donors and reinforces race and class hierarchies, is reaching its limits. This model, rooted in scarcity mindset and transactional fundraising practices, does not feel good to the people involved, and it no longer incentivizes donors like it used to.

In the field, we have attempted to address giving and staffing as separate issues. To address the giving crisis, we focus on donor behavior, new scripts and templates, and improved messaging. To address the staffing crisis, we pursue individualized strategies to motivate fundraisers and manage workplace stress. Little of it seems to be working, and the downward trends are accelerating.

To fix the crises in the nonprofit sector, we have to start at the foundation: enabling fundraisers to do their job without falling into patterns of chronic stress and burnout. Working together to improve the well-being of fundraisers will improve the capacity, impact, and productivity of the entire organization, as well as the sector as a whole. Being open to new strategies that challenge scarcity mindset and the constraints of transactional fundraising are the first steps toward righting the wrongs across the sector.

2

Show Me the Money (But Don't Talk About It)

I first learned about the concept of scarcity mindset when reading Lynne Twist's work. For more than 40 years, Twist has been a recognized global visionary committed to alleviating poverty, ending world hunger, empowering women and girls, supporting social justice, and promoting environmental sustainability. She is a cofounder of Pachamama Alliance and founder of the Soul of Money Institute. Almost 20 years ago, *The Soul of Money* (2006) changed the trajectory of my life and it still inspires the work I do today.

I picked up the book on my nightstand late one night after an exhausting day of spinning my wheels trying to prospect donors for a small education-focused nonprofit. At the time, I was searching for new ways to fundraise that would actually be sustainable. The unique way Twist talks about money, relationships, and values made me rethink how I approached my work. Once I started to understand how money shapes the world we live in and unconsciously affects every decision we make, I was able to question the power I was giving money in my own life.

In her book, Twist shares one story about giving back a check that has stuck with me all these years. She was offered money but then realized the giver wasn't in alignment with the organization's values at that moment in time. Rather than keep the significant amount of money, which would have been completely understandable given the good it could have done for her organization, Twist chose to give the money back to the donor.

I remember rereading that section several times. Something about that story finally made me realize that all money is not created equal, and money isn't the only thing of value. And so, it was a great honor when Twist agreed to join my podcast for an interview as a part of her book tour for *Living a Committed Life: Finding Freedom and Fulfillment in a Purpose Larger Than Yourself* (Twist and Chase 2023). In our conversation, Twist dropped several hard truths about scarcity and the movement of money in our society:

> We live in a culture that promotes scarcity. All the marketing, advertising, and everything that everybody engages in and receives promotes that you're not OK unless you acquire an item….These are the pain points. It's all designed psychologically to have us feel that we are in need of something to be complete and that we're incomplete without it. And that's not only in advertising and marketing; it's part of the monetary system.
>
> In truth, scarcity is an unconscious, unexamined mindset that's there before we even wake up in the morning. Even some global billionaires I work with are frantic to make more money. Why would anybody need more than $500 million or $10 billion? Why would someone still crave more? Because scarcity is a mindset. It's not rational. It's not related to reality. (Twist 2022)

Unpacking Scarcity Mindset

There is an important distinction to be made here between scarcity mindset and actual material scarcity. So many of us are underpaid, working paycheck to paycheck, and struggling financially. Our organizations are also often trapped in material scarcity, unsure if we will be able to cover payroll or make rent next month. Single-year grant cycles, one-time donations, and chronic low wages in our sector reinforce this material scarcity. This is real, pervasive, and not what I am talking about here. When I discuss scarcity mindset, I am talking about the patterns of thinking and behavior that lead us to believe there is not, and cannot ever be, *enough*. Enough money, enough time, enough staff, enough results. We have to hold two truths at once—we might be experiencing real scarcity in our lives, and we also might have adopted a scarcity mindset that holds us back in outsized ways and doesn't enable us to see a way forward.

I've had to learn difficult lessons about overcoming a scarcity mindset more than once, and I've committed to understanding how scarcity is consistently reinforced in our work through sector-wide beliefs and nonprofit training.

We hear it all the time—"We're a sector named after what we're not (*non*profit) as opposed to what we are" or "Nonprofit is a tax status, not a business model"—but regardless of these quips, these scarcity beliefs become ingrained in all of us. For some of us, the beliefs are explicitly taught in our workplaces and professional development training; and for others, we learn them implicitly through culture and social interactions. Whether we willingly and consciously "believe" these things or not, a scarcity mindset dominates nonprofit culture, and it's critical for us to address it.

From my personal experience and countless testimonies from clients, I see three main scarcity beliefs that shape our work.

Scarcity Myth 1: There Is Never Enough Money

This is the mistaken belief that there are neither enough donors nor ones with sufficient resources to meet our fundraising goals. This mindset breeds a sense of perpetual inadequacy, in which the potential for financial support feels far away and unattainable.

The stories we hear and tell within our sector are testament to this belief. Phrases like "There isn't enough money out there to support our mission" or "We don't have enough donors to raise *x* amount" are common to hear when talking to fundraisers and reflect deep systemic issues. For many of us, our beliefs about there never being enough money are reinforced by real-world challenges either personally or organizationally. However, the problem is often not the actual lack of funds available in the grand scheme, but the mindset that prevents organizations from seeing beyond these beliefs.

This scarcity belief affects how fundraisers approach their work. When we operate under the assumption that resources are limited, our strategies become constrained. When we expect that there will not be enough money, we unconsciously limit our fundraising by asking for less money than we need or taking money at all costs. This creates a self-fulfilling prophecy where we actually don't have enough because we didn't ask for it or because we said we could do it for less than we originally budgeted. When we're constantly thinking there isn't enough out there, we also start to focus on short-term wins to soothe our fears for the future instead of investing in long-term donor relationships or refreshed fundraising approaches. In doing so, we often narrow our focus further on a small pool of existing funders, neglecting the potential to explore new donor segments or to tap into neglected funding opportunities. At the end of the day, we can only raise the money we believe is out there to be raised.

Scarcity Myth 2: We Must Compete for Resources

I remember an old boss getting furious with me one time when I brought up our partnership with another nonprofit in a conversation with a funder. She was convinced that I sabotaged our funding because now the funder was going to be interested in the other organization, too. She was wrong. Although sometimes this is true with high-net-worth donors and their largest investments, it does not apply to the majority of fundraising efforts and is a disproportionately limiting view; even wealthy donors give to an average of five organizations in a given year (NPOInfo 2021).

This mindset often arises from the "fixed pie fallacy," a misconception that there is a fixed amount of wealth, so if one party gains, it's at the expense of another (Perry 2006). In the nonprofit sector, this can take the form of fundraisers believing that resources are finite and cannot change. This belief promotes the fear that if one organization wins, the other has to lose. But this isn't the case, and it isn't supported by research. Instead, most donors support multiple organizations and donor loyalty is not exclusive. According to a Gallup study, almost half of the donors (47%) give money to three to five organizations, and 15% give to six or more (Yu and Adkins 2016).

Because we know that funders are already giving to more than one cause, it doesn't make sense to waste our energy stressing about our donors' engagement in other organizations. Fundraisers who constantly see themselves in competition are often filled with self-doubt, concerned that donors will prefer other organizations. Fear of competition not only holds us back from finding opportunities for collective growth but it also affects our overall morale and motivation. If we constantly feel threatened, possessive of our donors, and afraid of their interest in other organizations, that is going to trap us in a constant state of stress that can lead to burnout, reduced productivity, and hindered innovation when it comes to donor engagement.

Scarcity Myth 3: We Should Operate with Minimal Overhead

A prevalent scarcity belief is that organizations must operate with the barest minimum of overhead costs. Although we often complain about this myth being imposed on us, we also extend it every time we boast about frugality as if it is a virtue in itself. Phrases like "We keep our overheads low to ensure more money goes to the cause" are often seen dropped into fundraising emails with an air of pride. This is more than just a budgetary decision or even a fundraising strategy; it reflects a deeply ingrained mindset that makes it seem like overhead takes away from our organization's integrity and mission.

In the Nonprofit Starvation Cycle, as reported by the *Stanford Social Innovation Review*, we see this problematic narrative highlighted:

> Our research reveals that a vicious cycle fuels the persistent underfunding of overhead. The first step in the cycle is funders'

unrealistic expectations about how much it costs to run a nonprofit. At the second step, nonprofits feel pressure to conform to funders' unrealistic expectations. At the third step, nonprofits respond to this pressure in two ways: We spend too little on overhead, and we underreport our expenditures on tax forms and in fundraising materials. This underspending and underreporting in turn perpetuates funders' unrealistic expectations. Over time, funders expect grantees to do more and more with less and less—a cycle that slowly starves nonprofits. (Gregory and Howard 2009, 50)

This narrative is particularly destructive because the opposite is true: essential investments in overhead—like staff development, infrastructure, and technology—are all critical for a nonprofit's long-term sustainability and impact. The Nonprofit Overhead Cost Study, a comprehensive research project by the Urban Institute's National Center for Charitable Statistics and the Center on Philanthropy at Indiana University, discovered alarming consequences of underfunding overhead: nonfunctional equipment, untrained staff, and outdated resources, all of which profoundly affect the organization's strategy, effectiveness, and mission delivery (Hager et al. 2004).

I understand that it's challenging to push back on donors or feel like you're one of the few organizations acknowledging overhead costs while other nonprofits run campaigns touting that "100% of the donation goes to X." However, here's what I've discovered over the years: although a few funders are fixated on overhead, many donors are far more interested in their personal relationships and engagement with the nonprofit and the demonstrable impact of their donations. This is where we have a lot more influence than we think we do.

As fundraisers, every time we take pride in our frugality or low overhead, we perpetuate the dangerous misconception among donors and the public that the lower the overhead, the more effective and trustworthy the organization. This has an impact on the entire sector, but it also affects the fundraising in our organization. Each time we play into the overhead myth, we maintain a toxic power dynamic and devalue everything inside our organization that makes the work possible. Plus, once we start to train our donors to look closely at our overhead and we make it seem like it is their job to "oversee it" in a paternalistic way as if they know best, we are just putting future pressure on ourselves to present an unrealistic picture of our operating costs.

All of these sector-wide beliefs lead to the deepening of scarcity mindset on the individual and organizational levels and set the stage for dysfunctional relationships between fundraisers and donors, distorting the power dynamics and causing a cascade of negative outcomes.

The Impact of Scarcity Mindset on Funder Relationships

Unaddressed scarcity mindset leads to a toxic power dynamic between fundraisers and funders where the desires and requirements of our funders are put above our own core mission and values. If we are constantly afraid that there isn't enough funding or funders, we hyper-focus on keeping our current or potential funders happy, even if it's at the expense of doing what's best for our organization in the long term. This fear-based relationship dynamic creates a substantial power imbalance, where funders have way too much influence because of our perceived dependence on their financial resources.

For years, I have had fundraisers tell me that they have a "strong relationship with a donor," but when I encourage them to negotiate with the donor or push back on an inappropriate request the donor is making, they tell me that they can't. So, what do we mean when we say we have a strong relationship with a donor? Do we mean they just give us money consistently? If we are constantly fearing the loss of support, that is not a strong relationship—that is a relationship steeped in scarcity mindset. If we aren't comfortable confronting, disagreeing with, or negotiating with our donors, it likely means we are accepting money at all costs even when there are conditions or terms that favor the donor's preferences over the organization's needs.

And so, the cycle continues: scarcity mindset affects donor relationships in ways that both deepen our limiting beliefs and move the relationships to become increasingly more transactional. And then we layer on fundraising teachings that overemphasize immediate results over sustainable strategies, ensuring that the urgent overtakes the important. This approach leads us to prioritize short-term fundraising targets at the expense of our long-term vision, impact, and donor relationships.

All of this affects the internal dynamics of nonprofit organizations. The constant chase for funds results in a myopic focus, where the essential values of community building, donor connection, and mission alignment are overshadowed by the pressing (and fear-based) need to secure funds. Under this constant pressure, fundraisers understandably often get overwhelmed and lose sight of why we are doing this work in the first place.

Transactional Fundraising

I was indoctrinated in transactional fundraising from watching one of my bosses fundraise. In my 20s, I worked for an executive director who had a very narrow approach to donor relationships that was not just assertive; it bordered on aggressive. He had a tendency to undervalue and even demean donors, especially when they considered reducing their contributions. I remember vividly how he would react when this happened—his demeanor would shift dramatically to one of entitlement and self-righteous indignation, almost as if the donors owed him something.

His interactions with funders always had a transactional and bullying tone focused on the exchange of money beyond all other aspects of the relationship. This approach affected me more than I realized at the time. It influenced how I viewed and prioritized donor relationships. I absorbed this energy and philosophy, which led me to develop a belief system where I saw donors as ATMs. Money—and getting their money—became more important than anything else.

And so, when donors, who were deeply connected to our cause and sincerely believed in our work, made contributions that I perceived as less significant or less than what I thought they could do, I was upset. I remember feeling shocked and disappointed when one donor—Jeff—gave the lowest sponsorship level for an upcoming event. At that time, I saw it as a failure on my part, not realizing I was trapped in a transactional way of thinking, valuing his monetary contribution over all of the other ways he supported our organization.

Looking back, I recognize that this mindset was not of my own making. It was influenced heavily by the pressure, attitude, and behavior of my boss. But more importantly, it was a reflection of a broader issue in the sector—a chronic prioritization of money over everything else, the hallmark of transactional fundraising.

I think about *transactional fundraising* as the monetary exchange from funder to fundraiser without meaningful connection, alignment, or a real relationship. This approach prioritizes interactions with funders that lead to the fastest financial return, sometimes accepting funds under restrictive conditions or with disproportionate expectations. No matter what, money is the primary value in the relationship.

What's confusing for many nonprofit leaders is that we are continuously told to "not be transactional" and instead to focus on transformational relationship building. However, at the same time, a lot of fundraising training teaches transactional fundraising strategies because the focus is predominantly on meeting immediate financial targets. A lot of fundraising theories have tried to thread this needle—to find the balance between focusing on the money versus focusing on relationship building. But when unaddressed scarcity beliefs are woven into the fabric of what we do, from the key performance indicators we track to how we evaluate fundraising health as a sector, there are too many norms and lessons that continue to lead to transactional fundraising.

The Road to Transactional Fundraising

My days as a fundraiser always began and ended the same way: glued to my email. On Monday mornings, I crafted and sent about 20 personalized emails to potential funders. After dispatching these messages, I'd briefly set my computer aside for a meeting, only to return an hour later, hopeful for signs of engagement. More often than not, none came. This cycle—filled with the hopeful anticipation of a response, the adrenaline surge at the sound of an incoming email, followed by the plunge of disappointment when it wasn't a reply—repeated itself regularly. By day's end, the silence felt like a personal insult.

The pattern of my week was predictable. By Wednesday, I might have received one or two responses, far from the success I had hoped for (especially considering the anxiety-inducing hours wasted on this strategy). By week's end, I was lucky to have one donor meeting on the calendar. By any measure, this was a broken strategy.

Despite these underwhelming outcomes, my dwindling confidence, and low conversion rates, I remained convinced that more hours and more emails would eventually translate into more donors. This belief stemmed from my training, yet it clashed with the disappointing reality I faced daily.

I remember one day sitting at my desk, clicking refresh on my email, just praying that a response would come through. I couldn't motivate myself to do any other work or move forward with other fundraising tasks because I was convincing myself that a response was just around the corner. In hindsight, I think I was in protection mode, hiding in my inbox because I was feeling so vulnerable and tender with all of the outreach I had just done that clearly wasn't working.

I didn't understand. I was following the script. I put in the hours, meticulously scrutinizing every email, following the lead of my executive director, mentors, and fundraising coaches and consultants. How could I not think I was the problem? It took years to undo this belief, and it only came after I realized the problem stemmed from the systems and norms, not my efforts behind the computer.

There is a significant gap between how we are taught to do things versus the most effective way to move money into our organizations. I've narrowed it down to five transactional norms I learned as a rookie fundraiser that supported my ineffective and exhausting approach. Perhaps you're familiar with them as well.

Transactional Norm 1: Don't Talk About Money For years I thought "don't be transactional" meant "don't talk about money." This led to this constant awkward feeling where I was meeting with donors to understand their priorities but was avoiding being too explicit about investment. But discussing money is part of our job, and there's a way to talk about money without being transactional— where the topic of investment is deeply rooted in shared values, hopes, and dreams. However, what makes a relationship transactional is when we care only about the person's money. When we value funders solely for their financial contribution, all of our interactions inherently become transactional. No one wants to feel like a human ATM.

This shows up in donor meetings where the conversation may never touch on money, yet the underlying intent is to try to figure out how to get the donor to give you money. I remember meeting with a huge donor of an organization similar to the one I was running. I knew that she loved the work of our organization and often read our educational materials. I took her out to lunch at our board chair's request. I was told to "build a relationship with her" and learn what she liked and didn't like about our organization. I was also told to see if there were any hints as to whether she might give us money in the future. But I was explicitly instructed not to bring up money. I went into the meeting thinking about money while simultaneously doing everything I could not to talk about it. Then, after the meeting, the board chair insisted I follow up with a thank you for lunch and an ask. I didn't want to do it because I knew it would feel completely out of the blue after the lunch we just had, but I followed orders. Needless to say, she did not fund us.

These types of meetings create disingenuous relationships because there is an underlying motive and incentive for interactions never directly discussed before or during the engagement itself (though often the donor still feels the elephant in the room). But even if we don't follow the meeting with an awkward email request for funding, or ever explicitly discuss money, an interaction can be transactional when there is a one-dimensional exchange that overlooks genuine connection because we are laser-focused on the person's money.

Transactional Norm 2: Focus on the Rolodex　　I have sat in so many board meetings where, at some point, the executive director or development director asked the board to "open up their Rolodex." Essentially, they are trying to create a list of donor prospects from the networks of their board members, and they might say they are trying to find people who are interested in the work of the organization. However, everyone in the room understands they are asking one thing: whom do you know who has money?

The board members uncomfortably mention a few names, and the next day the staff starts a mass-outreach campaign. There are a few primary problems with this approach. Not only does it leave many people behind, but "for too long, nonprofits and the like have relied on wealth as the key metric for predicting someone's willingness to give. But this limited transactional approach is at the root of the decline in American giving" (Crimmins 2022, xiii).

Focusing solely on wealthy prospects negates one of the most important elements of building donor relationships: do they actually care about our cause? Are they aligned with our mission and values? We get starry-eyed around the "friend with money" and forget to figure out if the relationship makes sense to both the funder and the organization. The problem isn't asking for introductions or reaching into our networks to connect with people we know; warm connections can be really helpful. The issue is how we are focused on that network through a money-only lens.

Having a board member make an introduction to a wealthy friend without clarifying why that friend would be particularly (and genuinely) interested in the work you are doing makes it clear you are focused on their money. Donors can feel that and understandably don't respond because they either aren't interested in the work of the organization or they don't see an opportunity for partnership because alignment isn't made clear through messaging. If you are a fundraiser and you're getting a low outreach response, particularly from warm connections, this is likely the reason why.

Transactional Norm 3: Emulate a Car Salesperson Years ago, a fundraiser with 10 years of experience shared something during a meeting that stuck with me. She said, "Sometimes fundraising just makes me feel like a car salesperson."

I couldn't shake her reflection because it resonated with me, too. I had often felt similarly. It made me ask myself, why does fundraising make us feel like a car salesperson? And why do car salespeople make many of us uneasy in the first place?

Even for those who've never directly dealt with pushy car salespeople (because let's acknowledge, some are fantastic!), the stereotype is familiar. The quintessential salesperson is desperate to sell us a car, regardless of whether or not the car is right for us. This image is precisely why many of us do extensive research before setting foot in a dealership, wary of trusting the salesperson to prioritize our needs.

There are a lot of parallels in traditional donor cultivation methods that lack transparency and sincerity. It appears in the form of impersonal, cold emails, where our motives remain unclear, and manifest in listening tours with potential donors, where our true intent—gauging their financial capacity—is cloaked in ambiguity. Whenever we place dollars over relationships, ignoring signs that a funder isn't a great long-term partner, we're sending the signal that we care about the same things as a car salesperson: getting their money, and nothing else.

Transactional Norm 4: Do More to Raise More Doing more, and running even more fundraising initiatives, doesn't make you an effective fundraiser; it makes you a tired fundraiser. Although it's crucial to diversify funding, a common misconception in the sector is that a successful fundraiser must continuously engage in a bunch of different fundraising activities. Some examples include organizing events, managing monthly giving programs, coordinating corporate volunteer days, processing cryptocurrency donations, and initiating influencer campaigns. Although each of these has the ability to effectively contribute to a fundraising strategy, if you try to undertake all of these strategies at once (particularly when faced with limited resources, staff, or time) you are not going to do any of them well.

I remember fundraising for a $200,000 organization with three staff members, and we were doing everything from galas and grant writing to chocolate, T-shirt, and coffee sales. None of our strategies were realized to the fullest because of our scattered spray fire approach. If I'm honest, this diversification was my attempt to find roundabout ways of raising money (like those chocolate, T-shirt, and coffee sales) and quick solutions (random events or urgent campaigns) over the development of long-term, genuine connections with donors that required vulnerability. That was when I first realized an increase in fundraising activities didn't necessarily equal an increase in revenue.

Plus, this "more is more" approach burns funders as much as fundraisers because it focuses on immediacy and surface-level engagement with donors. Relationships with donors become secondary to fundraising tactics and strategies that actually risks undermining the donors' trust, the organization's reputation, and ultimately compromises the sustainability and effectiveness of the fundraising strategies we're trying to implement in the first place.

Transactional Norm 5: Create Urgency No Matter What   We all see emails in our inbox with headlines like "Donate within the next 15 minutes or else *xx* happens!" or "10× your impact with your donation tonight!" Although these phrases are designed to capture attention, their long-term effectiveness is questionable, and they may even be detrimental.

Don't get me wrong; urgency created through relevance is a critical element in fundraising, such as when there is an upcoming deadline for an event or opportunity that requires your community's immediate attention. But our intent to generate urgency can be a double-edged sword. Many ways we have been taught to create immediacy in our sector advocate for a type of urgency that feels artificial or overly dramatic. Authentic urgency is a powerful motivator, but when it's fake, it can damage relationships with funders and prospects.

When we make exaggerated claims or use high-pressure tactics, it comes across as insincere and desperate while simultaneously overlooking the discernment and intelligence of our donors. Once again, the problem with this strategy is twofold: not only does it risk alienating potential donors in the short term but it also threatens to erode trust and credibility over time. When funders feel like they're being coerced or manipulated instead of being given an opportunity to make an investment they feel passionate about, it gets in the way of any chance of developing a genuine relationship in the future. Plus, overblown statements don't do our missions or our work justice by oversimplifying complex issues into soundbites. I understand that we have to be pithy at times and get our points across quickly, but we need to recognize when we've taken that too far and we're both disrespecting the donor and trivializing our work just to get a few more bucks.

Our outcomes always reflect our strategies. If we resort to tactics like clickbait campaigns, creating false urgency, incessant solicitation, and then swiftly moving on after a donation is made, we shouldn't be surprised by dwindling donor engagement and retention. Sure, we might get a one-time donation through guilt or pressure, but at what cost? How can we expect our donors not to feel exhausted by these tactics?

Moving Beyond Transactional Fundraising

If any of these transactional norms ring a bell, you're just like most fundraisers, myself included. This is how we were taught to fundraise or saw it modeled, so there's no need to feel embarrassed about implementing these strategies in the past. It's easy when you learn something new to beat yourself up for not knowing sooner, but that is not the point. As we've heard acclaimed writer Maya Angelou say, "Do the best you can until you know better. Then when you know better, do better."

It's time for us to acknowledge we've been recycling "best practices" in fundraising for years that yield mediocre results. Even worse, when we aren't raising the funds we need to, we don't switch it up, we just do more of the stuff that isn't working. These practices are contributing to the decline in giving and our horrible experiences fundraising. In a survey conducted in 2019 by The Harris Poll on behalf of *The Chronicle of Philanthropy* and the Association of Fundraising Professionals, 1,035 respondents (all *Chronicle* and AFP members) found, "There is a significant amount of tension and pressure in most fundraising jobs. Eighty-four percent feel tremendous pressure to succeed in their role, and more than half (55 percent) feel or have felt under-appreciated in their role. This pressure leads to 51 percent of respondents indicating they are very or somewhat likely to leave their current job over the next two years" (Association of Fundraising Professionals 2019).

Since the early 2020s, I've consistently seen fundraisers afraid of not having enough funds, enough donors, or enough capacity to raise the money they need. And because of their entrenchment in the historical, transactional fundraising model, they often try and fail to meet their goals. This model, deeply rooted in the scarcity mindset that Lynne Twist so eloquently spoke about at the beginning of this chapter, inevitably leads to diminishing returns. It affects financial contributions and donor retention, and equally critical and related, it affects the experience and well-being of the fundraisers themselves. Twist's wisdom reminds us that not all money is created equal, and the relentless pursuit of funds, fueled by a belief in never having enough, can lead us astray from our core values (Twist 2022). Therefore, as we move away from a scarcity-driven approach toward one of values-based alignment, we recognize the need for a fundamental shift in how we approach nonprofit fundraising. This shift is vital for the development of sustainable, impactful, and ethical fundraising methods, and it depends on us as fundraisers.

Historically, we have focused changes in fundraising on the donor, using behavioral science and psychology to understand, predict, and inspire donor behavior without holistic consideration of the preceding fundraiser behavior. However, as discussed in the introduction, donor behavior is a lagging indicator in giving, and fundraiser behavior is the leading indicator. Because fundraisers lead conversations, initiate relationships, build motivation, and provide prompts, the key to fundamentally changing fundraising lies in the behavior of fundraisers. This requires us to support fundraisers in shifting away from transactional methods that no longer align.

This might feel obvious to some, but we aren't acting like this in the sector. The metrics we primarily track for fundraising health are related to the donor, not the fundraiser. Furthermore, we haven't looked close enough at what drives or inhibits our behavior and actions as fundraisers. It's this key that can shed light on solutions moving forward.

Unfortunately, behind the desktops and task lists are human beings grappling with mounting discomfort and stress—overwhelmed and exiting the sector in large numbers. We are not just burned out; we're leaving a profession we once loved. This exodus is not a failure of the fundraisers, but a symptom of deeper issues within our sector. A sector-wide lens is critical because otherwise, every fundraiser believes that our discomfort and resistance fundraising is unique and our fault. For years I thought I must be a bad fundraiser because I wanted to throw up before every donor meeting. After connecting with more than 60,000 fundraisers, I can assure you that was not a personal failing but a result of a broken system. This is particularly true for Black and Brown fundraisers of color. As Rachel D'Souza, founder and principal at Gladiator Consulting, reminded me in a conversation on the *What the Fundraising* podcast, "Oftentimes those who are marginalized or have identities where they could be oppressed, they don't have a choice in the tactics of resilience" (D'Souza 2024). The way we fundraise is broken, and it is up to all of us to fix it. We need to confront this extreme discomfort, stress, and burnout on both individual and systemic levels to pave a path forward for a sector in crisis.

Case Study: Ben Houghton

How Dismantling Old-School Fundraising Helped Him Raise $1 Million (and Actually Enjoy New Year's Day)

"I used to think that fundraising had to have an ick factor," said Ben Houghton, a former participant of the Power Partners Formula™. "And this ick made me feel so gross, resistant, and overwhelmed about how to bring money into my organization. To raise money, I used to throw concerts and just pray. Like, pray the right donors would find us, and pray that they would feel connected to us, and pray that they would give.

And yes, that worked for a while, but that's not a sustainable fundraising strategy. I was at a total loss for how to do things. I used to dread the end of the fiscal year because then I would have to do it again."

That was where Ben was when I met him. But, despite the overwhelming nature of the work, Ben's devotion and love for Broadway for Arts Education, the nonprofit he cofounded in 2018 and currently leads, was evident. His enthusiasm and pride are clear when you talk to him about how his employees bring together the Broadway community and underserved youth to harness the transformative power of arts education and dismantle systemic barriers to success.

Ben worked his tail off day in and day out for his organization, and he facilitated important and impactful work. But it still never felt like enough. He was chronically stressed, burnt out, and second guessing everything he did. "I was very much living in scarcity and suffering from imposter syndrome," he says, all of which trapped him in a state of exhaustion and kept his organization from reaching its potential.

Why was Ben, like so many other fundraisers, deeply uncomfortable and unable to see a light at the end of the proverbial tunnel?

"I come from a performing arts background that exists in a complete scarcity mindset," Ben admits. This often made him feel like he couldn't say no to any funding opportunity because nothing else would ever come along. He simply could not walk away even if what the funder wanted wasn't the right fit for his organization.

Understanding there's more than enough money to go around—and he had all the skills and tools he needed to raise seven figures (or more!)—was part of unraveling his scarcity mindset. He also started to understand that the way you get to those big numbers is by pursuing the *right* opportunities—ones aligned with your organization's mission and values. And this means that sometimes you have to say no.

I think Ben said it best: "Sometimes you need to let stuff go so new stuff can grow."

And that's precisely what happened for Ben once he was able to approach fundraising with an eye toward alignment. His organization has grown substantially, benefiting from foundation grants, government support, and funding from individuals who are committed to the work he is doing with youth and are supportive of his mission to achieve transformational outcomes.

Ben used to fall prey to what I call the "hamster hustle wheel." He worked frantically on crafting dozens of perfect emails, posting more social media, prospecting (even more) donors, and planning all the events. We're told we need to do more if we want to raise more.

What actually brought Ben the most success was not targeting everyone, but "being really strategic" and recognizing that donors weren't just giving to his organization, they were receiving tremendous benefit as well. He figured out the assets his organization has to offer and found the donors who would benefit from and value those assets.

(continued)

(continued)

Now, instead of trying to prospect every single potential donor, Ben actually tries to do less. He's gotten better at saying no, recognizing when it's beneficial for both him and a potential donor *not* to move forward with a relationship. That way, he can release those donors to find the right organizations for them, and he can honor his time by finding and working with Power Partners. Turns out that doing less can actually be a win-win.

Old-School Fundraising	Alignment Fundraising
$200,000 Organization	$1,000,000+ Organization
You have to find more donors.	You have to find the *right* donors.
Fundraising is an ask, and you're a bad fundraiser if you aren't getting a yes.	Fundraising is an *offer,* and you only want a "yes" if it's the *right* "yes."
"Oh my God, I raised $__. How am I ever going to do that again?"	"Oh my God, I raised $_____. I can't wait to see how much I raise next year!"

3

This Job Feels Awful

I used to spend an excruciating amount of time on my organization's newsletters. I obsessed over the word choice, the font, the images, the links—every piece. I scrutinized the style, the descriptions of our campaigns, and the calls to action. I remember agonizing over every negative response we received; it was difficult to focus on the positive because I was so worried about bothering or upsetting our donors.

After one particular newsletter, I was confronted with the back-lash I dreaded: two seething emails from subscribers indignant at my audacity to ask for money. One reader chided, "You shouldn't be asking for money right now. Are you oblivious to what's going on with the economy?" Another said, "This is in such poor taste. Don't you realize we're all struggling right now?"

My stomach sank, and I felt like hiding under my desk. For a moment, I believed that it was truly inappropriate for me to invite people to donate to my organization. I wondered once again whether I should just quit fundraising altogether. And that was not the last time I felt embarrassment or discomfort from my role.

Discomfort is a feeling in our body that might resonate as a twinge or small resistance. I have accepted that a certain amount of discomfort and fear will always come with raising money because fundraising work is vulnerable and involves the risk of rejection. Certain discomfort does not have to be a roadblock; sometimes, it can be a guidepost that lets us know when we are stretching ourselves and taking risks that can lead to growth, learning, and alignment. Prioritizing our long-term alignment over short-term discomfort, whether our own or others', is a form of self-care because we are making the best decision for our future selves and who we want to be. For example, although it might be uncomfortable in the short term to have a hard conversation with a donor about overhead, it's a lot more problematic in the long run to accept funding with restrictions that make it hard for you to effectively run your organization. When I experience a healthy dose of discomfort, I know I'm challenging myself. This is the type of discomfort I hope you experience while reading some of the hard truths in this book.

However, we need to differentiate this type of regular, everyday discomfort from discomfort caused by an unsafe environment or individuals exhibiting racist, sexist, ageist, or other negatively motivated behavior. Toxic fundraising environments should not be treated like a growth edge or an opportunity to build resilience. Fundraisers often experience discomfort related to gender, including patronizing behavior and sexual harassment. And for fundraisers of color, there are additional external barriers as well. A report by Cause Effective, an organization focused on nonprofit sustainability, found that fundraisers of color experience higher levels of discomfort because of systemic racism and from being estranged by board members and executive directors who treat them as outsiders. The report states, "The very fabric of fundraising deals with discomfort, rejection, and often unrealistic expectations; inserting a racial component adds an extra hurdle to an already-charged interaction" (Daniel et al. 2019, 11).

All fundraisers need to understand when we are experiencing all forms of discomfort because it affects how we show up in our daily work and can indicate early signs of stress and burnout. Certain types of discomfort can quickly devolve into panic or chronic dysregulation, causing us to cease being effective at whatever we are attempting to accomplish. When fundraisers participate in the habits of transactional fundraising, I see them experience discomfort that often escalates to chronic stress or burnout.

From Discomfort to Burnout

I hear a lot of similar stories about burnout from clients. To make it easier for us to understand, let's imagine Nia. Nia, a fundraiser at a midsize environmental nonprofit, initially thrived on the challenges of fundraising. She felt some level of discomfort asking for money, but she approached it as a professional growth opportunity rather than an obstacle. When her boss told her to start raising money faster, the discomfort increased, but she kept trying to push it away and just "get over it."

The pressure began to mount in ways Nia hadn't anticipated. She was the only fundraiser for her organization, and everyone relied on her. She had too many disconnected tasks and was constantly bouncing from one thing to another, saying, "I feel like I spend a lot of time in survival mode because I don't have security or stability."

Nia's turning point came during a particularly demanding fundraising campaign. The target was ambitious, and the team was counting on her. Every rejection felt personal, not just a no to the ask but to her and the mission that was so important to her. As the campaign progressed, so did her stress. Nia found herself working longer hours, yet the sense of accomplishment she once felt was replaced by exhaustion and nagging thoughts like, "I am bad at fundraising. I can't do this."

Nia's story isn't unique. So many people in the sector have unknowingly crossed the line from discomfort to stress and then to burnout. Fundraisers often express feelings of being overwhelmed by the magnitude of their responsibilities. One of my surveyed fundraisers shared, "At my worst, I feel like I will let down my whole organization and that if it falls apart, it's on me."

Additionally, the constant pursuit of funding can lead to a state of chronic stress; as another fundraiser described, "I am always afraid of the 'no.' In this profession, I've been told I should not take these things personally, but when you love your organization and mission, any rejection just feels too personal." This fear of rejection, coupled with a deep commitment to the cause, often results in fundraisers internalizing the outcomes of our efforts, and if left unchecked, this spiral can (and often does) result in burnout. The challenge lies in managing these pressures while prioritizing personal well-being.

Part of this requires that we separate the normal discomfort that comes with fundraising from the pervasive chronic stress and burnout in the sector. Fundraising is inherently vulnerable and therefore uncomfortable, and as we know, some discomfort indicates growth and an opportunity for alignment.

Beyond the different types of discomfort, there is a distinct and meaningful difference across discomfort, chronic stress, and burnout. If not addressed, one state can easily escalate to another. Table 3.1 explores how these experiences are related.

Table 3.1 From Discomfort to Burnout

Discomfort	You might feel resistance to doing the task, particularly if it's outside of your comfort zone. You avoid things on your to-do list and feel occasional tightness in your stomach and throat when you complete certain tasks. You might experience some stress but it is manageable.
Chronic Stress	The tightness in your stomach no longer disappears; it feels like a constant companion. You feel more irritable and anxious and like you've lost your creativity and problem-solving skills. It's difficult to unwind at the end of the day and your mind spirals around your to-do lists, fundraising goals, and other work tasks.
Burnout	It becomes nearly impossible for you to do your assigned tasks given the level of emotional, mental, and physical exhaustion. Focusing is difficult, and you may even self-sabotage projects. You've lost your passion for the work and feel a deep sense of disconnect and dread with your responsibilities. You frequently experience thoughts of quitting.

Although these experiences aren't unique to fundraisers, we are susceptible to experiencing a rise in stress levels and corresponding symptoms because of the pressure we experience from our responsibilities. Awareness of intensification is key to avoiding burnout. When we can learn more about what is involved in each phase, we can help prevent escalation.

What Causes Discomfort?

Discomfort is very common among fundraisers and anyone involved in fundraising. Fundraisers are highly susceptible to discomfort because we are regularly asked to go outside our comfort zones to make big asks of potential funders or groups. When humans are asked to face rejection, high expectations, and the uncertainty of fundraising, it is to be expected that we experience some type of discomfort.

Discomfort can be manageable, but eliminating it completely is an unrealistic goal. It's OK to feel some discomfort when in new or intimidating situations. When navigating discomfort, the goal is to understand the root of the discomfort and interpret the body's messages correctly.

For the purposes of this book, let's focus on the three primary catalysts for fundraising discomfort:

- Discomfort that is activated any time we talk about the highly stigmatized topic of money or we put ourselves out there in vulnerable ways, like asking for help and risking rejection. A certain level of this discomfort will happen no matter which fundraising practices we use because fear is involved. (I still experience this type of discomfort sometimes when inviting people to donate.)
- Discomfort that comes from prioritizing alignment with our inner knowing over our short-term comfort or safety. This discomfort can be activated by circumstances like a lack of familiarity, initiating important but hard conversations, changing inequitable fundraising practices, or setting boundaries, all of

which are also an important part of prioritizing our long-term alignment over the short-term comfort of ourselves and those around us.

- Discomfort that comes from being out of alignment, usually stemming from transactional fundraising methods and scarcity mindset. We know the tactics we're using feel cringy and wrong, but we keep trying to "make it work" anyway. This adds stress and discomfort to situations where we feel like we need to put on a show instead of showing up honestly and authentically. This type of discomfort is a slippery slope to chronic stress and burnout.

I discussed the issue of discomfort with Dr. Ethan Kross, author of *Chatter: The Voice in Our Head, Why It Matters, and How to Harness It* (2021a). He explained discomfort is not inherently negative, and we should not aim to always avoid it. He said, "It is useful to experience a small jolt of anxiety or even a medium jolt before doing something consequential that's new. That anxiety motivates you to do what you need to do. . . . What we don't want, of course, is to have those negative emotions morph into chronic chatter, which then makes it hard to do what we want to do. One of the reasons why chatter is so toxic is it consumes us. It doesn't leave any attention for us to focus on the things we need to focus on: our jobs, our presentations, our kids, and so forth" (Kross 2021b).

As Kross explained, the key is to prevent the escalation of discomfort into chronic chatter or stress, which can then escalate into burnout (Kross 2021b). We'll dive deeper into managing our limiting beliefs, imposter syndrome, and self-doubt in the rest of the chapters, but for now we can understand how discomfort can spiral into negative mind frames.

Types of Stress and Chronic Stress

Chronic symptoms can arise from three types of stress. *Acute physical stress* can be triggered by a bad injury, starvation, or a perceived threat. To survive that threat, your body will activate your stress response (Chu et al. 2022). The acute stress response is a finely tuned physiological reaction that prepares the body to face immediate threats or challenges. At the core of this response lies the part of our brain that releases hormones that orchestrate the fight-flight-freeze reaction.

The physiological fight–flight–freeze reaction is our nervous system's response to a perceived harmful event, attack, or overall threat to survival. It triggers a whole host of subconscious activities in the body, like an increased heart rate and rising blood pressure (Chu et al. 2022). It is important to note that the acute stress response is tailored specifically for short-lived, immediate stressors. Once the perceived threat subsides, a feedback loop is activated, swiftly restoring the body to a state of equilibrium (Chu et al. 2022).

Chronic physical challenges indicate longer periods of stress. These can include natural disasters, long-term health conditions, or exposure to environmental hazards. It will trigger the same bodily reactions as acute stress, but the bodily response remains activated.

Psychological and social disruptions refer to stress created by thoughts about future events, past experiences, or even current circumstances. A thought can trigger the same biological response as an immediate or long-term threat (Barrett 2021b). Our body might not know the difference between a donor saying no and someone running at us with a knife. Though the specifics vary by individual, our bodies can react in very similar ways regardless of the stressor. If we are perceiving a threat, our stress response will turn on.

Regulation and *dysregulation* have become buzzwords when it comes to stress and stress management, and both refer to the nervous system. We'll talk more specifically about the nervous system later in this chapter, but to understand the transition from stress into chronic stress, it's helpful to clarify that *chronic dysregulation* refers to the inability to effectively manage or regulate emotional responses. It represents a decline in our ability to cope with stressors effectively. A healthy and emotionally regulated person will and should experience some levels of stress and overwhelm—sometimes we need to be dysregulated, such as when we're angry at an injustice. However, when we experience these symptoms for extended periods of time—and do not have the ability to return to a baseline state—it leads to chronic stress.

Chronic stress is a "consistent sense of feeling pressured and overwhelmed over a long period of time," which most scientists and researchers define as several weeks (Yale University Medicine n.d.). Chronic stress often impairs our ability to cope with daily tasks and challenges. Over time, dysregulation and chronic stress can form a loop, where one can activate the other and continue the unhealthy cycle.

Most fundraisers I've come into contact with over the last few years feel stuck in chronic stress. Chronic stress can intensely interfere with productivity, relationships, and mental and physical health. For many of us, when more than several weeks pass without the ability to return to a calm state, we're escalating toward burnout.

Reaching Burnout

Burnout feels like being completely exhausted emotionally, mentally, and physically. It feels like we can no longer meet the constant demands at work or in our personal lives. Overall, it feels like being overwhelmed by everything. Burnout is so emotionally draining that it makes productivity and energy levels tank, and leaves individuals feeling increasingly helpless, hopeless, cynical, and resentful.

Burnout has severe effects on the individual, and these effects on fundraisers translate to issues in nonprofit organizations as a whole. According to the 2023 Nonprofit Workforce Survey, a staggering 50.2% of respondents identified stress and burnout as key factors contributing to workforce shortages in the nonprofit sector (National Council of Nonprofits 2023).

Discomfort to chronic stress to burnout is a vicious cycle, and it isn't the fundraiser's fault. First, the problematic transactional fundraising norms of our sector set fundraisers up for failure out of the gate. Then, organizations are unable to properly allocate resources to support their fundraisers who are under immense pressure, managing excessive workloads, and constantly overwhelmed.

These circumstances lead fundraisers to experience burnout, which then leads to the fundraisers leaving the nonprofit sector. These vacancies leave organizations with even fewer resources of support, and the cycle continues, spiraling into worsening conditions.

In *The Happy, Healthy Nonprofit: Strategies for Impact Without Burnout*, authors Beth Kanter and Aliza Sherman (2016) describe the stages of stress specific to nonprofit conditions as a journey from being passion-driven to passion-depleted. Nonprofit employees and leaders enter the sector fueled by a passion to do good and to help their communities, but because of a culture centered on self-sacrifice and neglect of personal well-being, these organizations pile on relentless demands with scarce resources, driving fundraisers to do more with less. This progression leads to a decline in fundraisers' physical and mental health and, eventually, a complete depletion of their passion and drive.

Dr. Linnea Passaler is a recognized authority on nervous system dysregulation, a sought-after speaker, and the founder and CEO of Heal Your Nervous System (which is also the title of her book). Passaler says that burnout robs people of their purpose. "Burnout is where people quit their jobs," she says. "Burnout is particularly potent for nonprofit folks because nonprofit people do the work they do because they are so connected to a greater sense of purpose. They do the work they do because they believe in the work. When nonprofit folk experience burnout, they feel a loss of their identity" (Passaler 2023).

Passaler explained that burnout can hurt those of us working in nonprofit organizations, particularly because "burnout makes people a cynic. This shift is more likely for people with highly sensitive nervous systems, who tend to be motivated by big causes. It is in the people who have a great sense of purpose in life, who often are attracted to mission work like nonprofits. They are the ones who are most at risk for developing burnout. It makes people emotionally disconnected. And it's not that fundraisers don't care about the cause anymore, but it's the fact that burnout fundamentally changes your brain and body" (Passaler 2023).

I already knew that as nonprofit professionals we deeply connect our identity to our work, but to learn that we are particularly susceptible to burnout, which can then reduce our sense of purpose, was powerful. This knowledge further motivates me to transform our jobs and our sector.

When I felt burnt out, I started to understand how important it is for us to shift our approach to enabling fundraisers. Once we are candid about the underlying issue, we can begin the conversation about designing adequate solutions to support fundraisers.

Countdown from Discomfort to Burnout

This is the countdown to burnout that I've seen play out among too many fundraisers.

4. Initial discomfort fundraising. In the early stages of fundraising, fundraisers might experience mild stress, fear, or discomfort. This discomfort could look like the following:

- Feeling nervous about achieving a fundraising goal
- Feeling overwhelmed by the number of funders we need to reach out to
- Feeling anxious about navigating team dynamics
- Feeling frustrated or defeated by the transactional methods that escalate discomfort

3. Stress and dysregulation. If initial discomfort goes unaddressed, or is a result of misalignment or transactional fundraising methods, we may be unable to manage our emotional responses. Continuous pressure and increased fear can lead to the following:

- Irritability and anxiety over fundraising goals
- Decline in our ability to cope with demands and fundraising expectations
- Decline in our ability to connect with donors

2. Chronic stress. If early challenges, stress, and dysregulation in fundraising are not addressed and resolved, fundraisers may enter into chronic stress. In chronic stress, the fundraiser will experience the following:

- Physical symptoms like headaches and sleep disturbances
- A decrease in work efficiency and our ability to perform fundraising tasks
- An inability to build and maintain healthy relationships

1. Complete fundraiser burnout. Unmanaged chronic stress in fundraising can culminate in burnout, which results in the following:

- Feeling like we're drowning in the onslaught of demands
- Feeling emotionally exhausted
- A significant decrease in productivity and enthusiasm for the mission
- Perfectionism or paralysis that halts effective donor communications

Elements of Fundraising That Lead to Burnout

From my experience, surveys, and research, I've identified a number of elements of fundraising and sector norms that contribute the most to burnout: pressure, power dynamics, uncertainty, rejection, and isolation. These emotional experiences affect the lives of fundraisers and the financial outcomes of our organizations because they drive our discomfort into burnout. To create solutions that support fundraisers, we need to first understand each of these experiences.

Pressure

There's an expectation of meeting ever-increasing goals consistently as a fundraiser. In my survey, one fundraiser shared their severe anxiety about failing to hit their CEO's benchmarks: "I always feel like the job never ends. You can never bring in enough money, and when you exceed expectations, your budget increases again. It's like a hamster wheel you can never get off."

Regardless of external circumstances or internal levels of support, fundraisers take the weight of responsibility on our backs and are expected to smile through the strain. The pressure often arises from the expectations and demands placed on us to meet specific performance standards, financial goals, or deadlines. High levels of pressure in professional settings have been identified as a significant stressor profoundly affecting our mental health and well-being (Bhui et al. 2016).

Our efforts to meet budget targets, organize events, and the hustle culture in the sector can move even the most grounded fundraisers beyond discomfort. Individuals subjected to chronic pressure might experience heightened levels of stress, anxiety, and burnout (Bianchi et al. 2015). The combination of big goals and tight timelines can create a persistent state of heightened arousal and tension that we often try to address by overworking, which only makes matters worse.

Raising money not only for the organization's mission but for our own salaries and the salaries of our peers further intensifies the pressure to overwork. When the body feels looming deadlines—especially ones that can affect our financial security—the brain starts pumping the body with the hormone cortisol, creating a physiological-biological response that heightens feelings of stress (Key 2015). We cannot just teach fundraisers coping skills to handle this pressure and stress; we also need to redesign fundraising to reduce stress and ultimately reject the norm of self-sacrifice.

Power Dynamics

Power dynamics are the subtle and intricate interplays that unfold within social, organizational, or hierarchical settings, where individuals or groups hold different levels of influence, control, and authority. These dynamics shape our interactions because of the way they determine how decisions are made and who gets to make them.

This can significantly affect individuals' experiences and well-being, particularly when power imbalances are pronounced.

In many nonprofits, power is disproportionately concentrated at the top, and decision-making processes are heavily influenced by donors or board members. This imbalance creates harmful power dynamics, particularly for fundraisers who face unique stressors and challenges as a result. Research indicates that perceived powerlessness or a lack of agency can contribute to feelings of helplessness and diminished self-esteem (Anderson and Berdahl 2002). The sense of powerlessness felt by fundraisers and staff is a precursor to burnout. Passaler noted that a lack of power also affects our productivity, "When you have a sense of powerlessness, you lack efficacy in your work" (Passaler 2023).

Additionally, identity and the power dynamics rooted in race, class, age, and gender hierarchies influence these fundraising experiences. This further reinforces the culture within fundraising that prioritizes donor preferences, a concern highlighted in "Money, Power, and Race: The Lived Experience of Fundraisers of Color" (Daniel et al. 2019). In the report, the Cause Effective team explained, "Belittlement happens as a matter of course in dealing with donors, board members, and, in some positions, executive staff" (Daniel et al. 2019, 13). Fundraisers of color regularly face biases and assumptions, and as one mid-career development staffer said, they have learned "to bite my tongue and not speak out, as that could lead to disagreements and loss or lack of funding" (Daniel et al. 2019, 13).

This culture of deference extends to the prioritization of the donor's comfort over the dignity and equity of fundraising staff. A mid-level fundraiser described the dilemma: "Oftentimes I'm raising money from people who are not like me, and having to navigate what the dynamic is. . . . How is that potentially connected to race, gender, and age? And how am I going to respond in the moment at the same time that I know that my goal is to raise money for the organization" (Daniel et al. 2019, 13).

Board members, as part of this hierarchy, often fail to support fund-raisers in these challenges. They can be both complicit in perpetuating these dynamics and reluctant to challenge their peers, further exacerbating the problem.

Uncertainty

"Uncertainty is the enemy of philanthropy," said Patrick Rooney, Research Director at the Center on Philanthropy at Indiana University (Rooney in Hagenbaugh 2008). When a significant portion of donations come at the end of each year (which is true for many organizations), it can be mentally draining to try to predict and plan for those numbers while trying to fill the gap throughout the year. This leaves us in a state of perpetual uncertainty. The anxiety of not knowing whether we'll hit our targets is a constant undercurrent, affecting not just our long-term strategies but also our day-to-day morale.

Stress typically arises when we perceive our available strategies and resources as insufficient to cope with a hard situation (that is, we don't have the resources we need to do our jobs or don't think we have the skills, strategy, or donors to reach our fundraising goal). Uncertainty involves the perception that a negative event might or might not occur with no definitive means of prediction (Dugas et al. 2001). Scarcity mindset can create additional negative perception and then the tension can be exacerbated by unexpected donor behavior. This often makes fundraising a balancing act between optimistic planning and the management of unpredictable resources.

Although fundraisers do influence donor behavior, we have no control over the environment that surrounds us and our donors. Because of this, a level of perceived uncertainty will always be a part of the job. However, when that uncertainty is connected to our financial stability and ability to support our cause, that uncertainty can lead to a state of chronic stress and burnout.

Those who struggle to cope with uncertainty are more likely to excessively worry and maintain an elevated state of anxiety (Birrell et al. 2011). These feelings of uncertainty and scarcity can lead fundraisers to experience intense fear and chronic stress about our ability to do our jobs, support our communities, and pay our colleagues' salaries. Furthermore, heightened intolerance of uncertainty tends to impede problem-solving abilities, leading to inaction, procrastination, indecision, and avoidance of ambiguous situations, which are all the things we need to be able to manage in order to create more secure funding (Chirumbolo et al. 2022).

The experience of uncertainty does not only have to do with how we are going to raise money. Another way uncertainty shows up in fundraising is ghosting, where a donor stops responding to communication. When we get ghosted, it leaves us wondering why we were abandoned and questioning what we did wrong. I spoke about this specifically with Britt Frank, licensed clinician, educator, and trauma specialist, and the author of *The Science of Stuck: Breaking Through Inertia to Find Your Path Forward* (2022a), and she explained that when we get ghosted, we often come up with a narrative about why we were left unanswered. And most often, we blame ourselves. We almost never blame the ghost (Frank 2022b).

Rejection

There is no fundraising without rejection. Even the most successful fundraisers in the world deal with many forms of rejection as we put ourselves out there in vulnerable ways. However, despite the normalcy of rejection, it's important to acknowledge its impact on fundraisers. Rejection feels awful, and can be a significant stressor, adding to self-doubt and imposter syndrome. One of my survey respondents said, "Even though I am a confident fundraiser, there is still doubt in every campaign. Is the messaging right? Are we messaging too often? Not enough?"

Rejection ranges from interpersonal rebuffs during social interactions to declined grant proposals or donors deciding not to invest. Each of these scenarios represents not just a missed opportunity for funding but also a personal blow to the fundraiser.

Mark Leary told the American Psychological Association in their report on the pain of social rejection, "People have realized just how much our concern with social acceptance spreads its fingers into almost everything we do" (Leary in Weir 2012). Research consistently highlights the profound effects of rejection on emotional and psychological states. "As researchers have dug deeper into the roots of rejection, they've found surprising evidence that the pain of being excluded is not so different from the pain of physical injury" (Weir 2012).

This experience of rejection can be further intensified by the nature of nonprofit work, where we are deeply connected to our work and the organization's mission is closely tied to our identity. A no can sometimes feel like a dismissal of our cause and personal rejection rather than just a professional setback. While getting a no is—and always will be—a part of fundraising, we need a way to cope with the rejection so that it doesn't intensify feelings of chronic stress and burnout.

Isolation

We are experiencing an epidemic of loneliness and isolation as a society, and multiple reports cite isolation as one of the major precursors to chronic stress and burnout (Office of the U.S. Surgeon General 2023). Beyond the large social and technological forces that drive isolation, oftentimes development teams are small groups of people, if not just one person. The lack of community and camaraderie can make it difficult for fundraisers to feel connected. Even when fundraisers have team members in other departments, we can still feel alone because of the burden and pressure of our job and the fact that other team members tend to try to distance themselves from fundraising.

Isolation also intersects with other common experiences of fundraisers, like self-doubt and rejection. It's been noted that feelings of rejection can lead to a "sense of social disconnection and loneliness" (Longa et al. 2021). When we are overworked, struggling sometimes as the only fundraiser in our organization, it can become difficult to muster the energy to connect with others, especially when asking for help or the ear of a colleague or friend can also feel like a vulnerable thing to do. We need to replenish our energy and spend time with people who love and support us, but when we're already on the cusp of burnout, being present for those connections can feel just as draining.

For fundraisers of color, there is another layer of their experience of isolation. Cause Effective interviewed fundraisers of color for their "Money, Power, and Race" report (Daniel et al. 2019, 18) to showcase their experiences. When these fundraisers were asked about their feelings on isolation, they responded with these comments:

- "I am often one of the few people of color in the room at some events, and have to navigate tricky circumstances and conversations. I have never had a POC supervisor, and often I am tasked with explaining why inclusion, diversity, and being intentional about historically oppressed communities is important, and how to do so."
- "If I am working with a conservative and wealthy board of older individuals, as a radical queer person of color, there is a disconnect that goes beyond board development and donor relations. There is genuine human disconnect."
- "I have no partners on the board to discuss equity issues from marginalized perspectives, much less drive an agenda, and due to the majority whiteness of my sector, little opportunity to connect with fellow POC leaders."

Feeling isolated can be a profoundly discomforting experience, given our biological desire for belonging (Cohen 2022). When racial stress is stacked on top of all the other elements of fundraising that lead to burnout, it's no wonder our colleagues of color are often feeling it hardest.

Some of the elements of fundraising that lead to burnout—like rejection and uncertainty—come with the territory. As we'll discuss further in Chapter 4, self-trust and inner alignment help us avoid burnout by guiding us through the more vulnerable parts of fundraising with self-confidence. But the other elements—pressure and overwork, power dynamics, and isolation—are a result of transactional fundraising methods, and are rooted in deep cultural issues present in the sector.

Stigma About Fundraising

My husband and I love watching TV shows that explore a variety of societal themes, from the challenges faced by individuals to the intricacies of relationships and community life. Often, these shows touch on the topic of fundraising, and it's disheartening to see how fundraising is frequently portrayed. The scenes are filled with clichés and misconceptions that spread negative stereotypes about our profession. I often find myself thinking, "This is exactly why our jobs are so challenging. There's so much stigma about raising money." *Stigma* is defined as "labeling, negative stereotyping, linguistic separation (the target is commonly referred to by a name), and power asymmetry" (Andersen et al. 2022, 847). In the nonprofit world, stigma sometimes comes from the misconception that our organizations are less professional or efficient compared to for-profit organizations, and feeds the idea that nonprofit work isn't real work. Fundraising is sometimes seen as an amateur or unskilled activity, relegated to small-scale events like bake sales or raffles, rather than being recognized as a sophisticated and strategic profession. Whether it's a bake sale or the Met Gala, the stereotype of the fundraiser is the haggard woman running around with the clipboard, obsessing over the biggest potential funder in the room, and forever hounding people to donate more.

The stigmas about fundraising in the nonprofit sector are intensified by societal and cultural norms about money. The pervasive belief that discussing money is taboo often leaves us understandably reluctant to initiate conversations about funding. A survey by the investment management group Capital Group found that "people are more comfortable talking about marriage problems, mental illness, drug addiction, race, sex, politics, and religion than they are about money. In fact, out of a dozen topics, men and women across all generations ranked household earnings, retirement savings, and debt as the tabooest" (Capital Group 2018).

Stigmas about the nonprofit sector and money converge to build societal beliefs that fundraising involves tricking or pressuring people into giving or that inviting people to donate is akin to begging. This stereotype makes it seem like fundraising is "bad," but calling it that is really just a reaction to our discomfort talking about money.

But why are fundraisers being stigmatized and stereotyped like this when we are actually a vital part of our societal fabric? Why has society overlooked how fundraisers move money to create the changes we want to see in the world and foster genuine, mutually beneficial relationships for everyone? Fundraisers have so much to offer and our work is sacred, but we are rarely recognized for the skills we bring to the table or the change we capacitate in the world.

Being a fundraiser can be a confusing experience filled with contradictions. We are judged primarily (if not solely) by the amounts of funds we raise, but are simultaneously told not to be transactional. We are told to build strong relationships, but aren't given the time, resources, capacity, or support to do so. We're constantly working to prove our worth and effectiveness, but rarely receive recognition due to the way society stigmatizes the work. With all of these conflicting expectations, can we blame ourselves for experiencing self-doubt and imposter syndrome?

This environment is counterproductive to the very essence of our jobs, and contributes significantly to the unfavorable circumstances that create discomfort and burnout. There are many elements of fundraising that exacerbate the situation—some inherent to the job and some perpetuated by transactional fundraising. Unfortunately, when we talk about problematic experiences in the sector and the stigma that surrounds us, we usually do it in silos and only on a surface level. We keep the conversations fairly superficial to get head nods of recognition in a room, but then we quickly flip to quick-fix tactics like transactional fundraising strategies and oversimplified recommendations to take paid time off or find a new self-care strategy. This isn't enough.

There continues to be a decline in satisfaction and fundraisers are leaving the sector more than ever (Haynes and Childress 2022).

I think we're spiraling around the same conversations because we believe we can solve these problems in our brains alone. We can't. Purely trying to outthink the problem doesn't go deep enough. That's why our tired solutions aren't working—they focus on the strategy instead of on our experience. Throughout my career, I had multiple cycles of hustling and grinding that would result in complete collapse (at least for a period of time). It was my final collapse that led to my deeper understanding of the problem at hand. When I began to grasp the relationship between my fundraising and my nervous system, I began to see the need for different interventions.

The Body's Response to Transactional Fundraising

In my 20s, I spent a lot of time at the doctor's office after a car accident. It was a fender bender, but the force of the collision slammed my head back into my headrest, giving me severe compression in my lower back. But years after that accident—and many trips to the chiropractor and acupuncturist—I still had pain. It was like my body wasn't my own anymore. I didn't know what was causing it or how bad it was going to get. I sought a neurologist and physical therapist but could not find a lasting remedy, and no one could explain why I continued to have chronic pain.

At the same time, I was going full-speed on the transactional fundraising hamster wheel. On the surface, it looked like I had it all together, but behind the scenes I was struggling with constant rejection and self-doubt. Day after day, I juggled appointments with doctors and donors, going from medical offices to coffee shops. I tried to focus on getting people to invest in my organization while my lower back was in constant pain.

When my fundraising budget doubled, the pain got so bad I couldn't get out of bed. I felt tension throughout my back and neck that escalated into numbness and tingling down my hands. There I was—young, eager, totally bedridden, and scared.

A friend recommended Dr. John Sarno's (1991) *Healing Back Pain: The Mind-Body Connection*. After more than 20 years treating back pain, Sarno realized that most back pain is not caused from structural abnormalities (herniated disks, misaligned spines) but rather is a trick the brain plays to disguise and distract from uncomfortable emotions like anger, sadness, not-enoughness, and anxiety.

Dr. Sarno's radical theory argued that instead of dealing with uncomfortable emotions, the brain causes the body to feel physical pain (Sarno 1991). Patients spend all their time managing physical discomfort rather than emotional discomfort because emotions are more difficult to handle. It suggested negative emotions could prompt the brain to present real physical pain. This resonated deeply with me, and after reading this work, I dove deeper into the mind-body connection Dr. Sarno described.

Finally, I found a plausible explanation for my inexplicable medical issues. My fears, resistance, and feelings of not enough-ness were manifesting physically, causing my body to experience pain. These struggles were a defense mechanism, a bodily response to my inability to confront my circumstances and emotions.

In writing this book, I went back and forth a lot about whether or not to talk about the brain-body connection because I'm not a therapist, somatic practitioner, or formally trained in neuroscience. I have decided to include this section of the book for two reasons:

- I hope that drawing these parallels in the research I have done inspires more research in this area. I hope we look more deeply at what is happening in the brain and body of fundraisers because in doing so, we move toward supporting fundraisers more holistically. On a discovery call with a potential client, a fundraiser said, "I want to work with you because you make fundraising feel so human." My heart sank because how on earth can this wholly relational activity be about anything else?
- I am also talking about the brain-body connection here because for many of us, we can't see a problem, or don't notice something

until it shows up in our body. I can't tell you the number of times I was hustling and in total chronic stress, but I didn't notice until I was sick and unable to work. There seem to be so many fundraisers dealing with chronic pain or other unexplained ailments and illnesses. Have you experienced this? If you have, you're not alone. Our body will often get our attention when it needs to and for that reason, I want you to have some insight into what it might be saying and why.

As we've said, all fundraising comes with some level of discomfort in the body because it requires vulnerability when asking for contributions, partnerships, or anything else. The brain will react to that discomfort in any way it knows how, including generating pain signals. I had to learn new ways to manage discomfort, and make sure I was not perpetuating the discomfort with transactional fundraising strategies so that my discomfort didn't turn into chronic stress and, ultimately, chronic pain. In doing so, I found unanticipated fundraising success both in how much I raised and, more importantly, how I felt as a fundraiser.

I want to highlight the connection between the specific stress experiences of fundraisers and our physical lives. Once we have a better understanding of the brain-body connection and its intersection with fundraising, we have even more opportunity to not only make fundraising more effective, but to actually make it feel good.

Fundraising and the Nervous System

I loved biology in school, but I wish we had delved deeper into the intricacies of the nervous system. Imagine if instead of memorizing cellular structures, we were taught how to connect the dots between our nervous system and our emotions, decisions, and interactions.

The *nervous system* is a network of specialized cells, known as neurons, that facilitates the transmission of information within the body. These neurons enable our brain to communicate with our body. The nervous system controls our movements, thoughts, and automatic responses (Institute for Quality and Efficiency in Healthcare 2016).

These neurons allow for swift communication between different body parts so we can perceive our surroundings, process data, and respond to a variety of stimuli. Have you ever stepped into a freezing cold shower and instinctively jumped back? That's our neurons firing a rapid message to our brain, alerting it to the sudden chill, and then our brain instantly reacts, advising us, "Get out of there! That water is way too cold!" Our brain is constantly searching our environment for anything that could be threatening to us. We'll dive more into how these messages from our nervous system can contribute to limiting beliefs in Chapter 4.

The nervous system is made up of the parasympathetic nervous system and the sympathetic nervous system. The *parasympathetic nervous system*, which activates during rest, plays a major role in our well-being (Cleveland Clinic n.d.). It not only helps us connect with others, communicate effectively, make decisions, and take action but also directs energy toward essential bodily functions like healing, digestion, and maintenance of our immune system.

Stress and stress responses are part of our *sympathetic nervous system*, which is responsible for turning on your fight-flight-freeze response (Cleveland Clinic n.d.). It is the alarm clock in your body that activates when a threat is found. When that alarm clock goes off, the human body shifts priorities from metabolically expensive activities like digestion and healing to sending energy to your muscles so you will have the necessary reserves to fight or flee.

The sympathetic nervous system operates unconsciously, responding to both acute and chronic stressors in milliseconds (Alshak and Das 2024). This biological mechanism, an effective evolutionary alarm clock, traditionally responded to immediate dangers. However, modern stressors differ; we no longer face threats like a lion chase, but instead we encounter social anxiety, fear of rejection, and perfectionism, among other psychological challenges. This stress, which activates the same response, persists in fundraising through tasks like sending high-stakes emails or calling a donor, and keeps us in a continuous state of alert. As a result, our bodies are unable to complete the stress response cycle, reengage the parasympathetic nervous system, and effectively return our body to a state of rest and digest.

Instead, we become paralyzed because, within the sympathetic nervous system, is a state called *freeze*, where mammals literally freeze their bodies and part of their cognitive functioning to play dead so they can avoid death when under attack (Roelofs 2017). Although physical attack is unlikely in the fundraising office, fundraisers still experience something popular science calls *task paralysis*, which occurs when people feel overwhelmed (Smith 2022). Instead of working through your to-do list like normal, you freeze, unable to make a decision or move forward. Ellen Hendriksen, a clinical assistant professor at Boston University's Center for Anxiety and Related Disorders, says the freeze response occurs when we have too much to do. That task list represents the "threat of failure, or it could be the threat of letting others down. It could be the threat of feeling stupid or incompetent because we don't know where to start or how to do things" (Hendriksen in Smith 2022). Task paralysis is also experienced at a higher rate by people with perfectionism, and people with perfectionism have a more difficult time engaging in stable interpersonal relationships.

Oscillating between this freeze response and a flight stress state that limits or inhibits effective and empathic communication can and will derail any fundraising initiatives.

Imagine this: on your very first day at your new nonprofit, you meet your boss, Aisha. Aisha is passionate about the organization's cause, enthusiastically explaining all of the initiatives and goals she's working toward. Her computer, however, is a mess—covered in open documents and internet tabs. When you look closely, the documents and tabs are all related to different fundraising initiatives—from Google ad grants, to virtual event planning, to grant submission portals—it's a lot. It becomes clear that although Aisha is trying a variety of tactics, she has not found an efficient strategy to raise money.

Aisha's approach—which is very representative of the current fundraising landscape—often activates the body's fight, flight, or freeze response. This can lead to what we've come to recognize as shiny object syndrome, where we're constantly looking for the next new fundraising answer, or to a state of paralysis, held back by perfectionism and fear of failure. When we get stuck in either of these states, we often start to feel overwhelmed and exhausted. We may also experience a sense of disconnection from our bodies, as though we're on autopilot, just going through the motions. This response, intended to protect us from immediate threats, often leads to a state of hyper-alertness, stress, and a perpetual cycle of reactivity. Although it's true that time is finite, and we all have too much to do, I believe the time management issues most fundraisers face are largely the result of this stress and reactivity, not our to-do list. Without the ability to prioritize activities that lead to sustainable fundraising success and identify what not to do, we cannot be the productive and effective fundraisers we want to be.

Task paralysis, perfectionism, and shiny object syndrome all create resistance, which inhibits our ability to take effective action. Plus, if we are in stress or burnout, it becomes nearly impossible to do the one thing fundraisers must do to succeed: build authentic relationships. Good fundraising cannot happen while the fundraiser's nervous system remains in a fight, flight, or freeze state. Instead, we want a healthy nervous system that oscillates between rest and stress— without getting stuck in stress.

Passaler (2023) broke this concept down clearly:

> The human nervous system is the filter through which we experience reality, both our external and internal reality. It's what generates our feelings, our emotions, and our thoughts, but it's also what directs everything in our body. And so, I like to use the analogy of a fern. A regulated nervous system (a nervous system that works well) is like a fern that flexes and flows under external stressors. So, it's not a nervous system that is always relaxed.
>
> It's completely fine to go into different states many times throughout the day. The point is to be able to go with the flow, just the flow of life, and follow those ups and downs in a way that does not feel chaotic and out of control. So, when we can embrace this idea of a flowing nervous system, a flexible nervous system, that means we can let go of this idea of perfection, of having everything under

control all the time. And that is actually what a regulated nervous system is—it's a nervous system that can quickly rebound under stressors. If we think about a nervous system that is overwhelmed, that is working beyond its capacity, that's when we feel powerless.

A common misconception about wellness and mental health is that we have to be happy or calm all the time. That's not the case. A well-regulated nervous system isn't characterized by the absence of stress, but rather by its capacity to effectively manage and adapt to stress. This flexibility is vital for maintaining our physical and mental health, and for sustaining our professional productivity and success. Without this capacity, fundraisers cannot do their jobs. The key lies in cultivating awareness of our natural stress responses, employing holistic tools to manage stress, and tackling systems and practices that exacerbate it. This will enable us to prioritize engaging in stressful but beneficial activities, like sending that fundraising email that's been sitting in our drafts folder, without the same risk of chronic stress and burnout.

A Recipe for Bad Fundraising

The causes of discomfort, dysregulation, chronic stress, and burnout in fundraising are clear. I wish that the dire state of the health and wellness of the fundraisers powering this ecosystem was enough to create change. It should be enough to see and hear about our colleagues, grantees, and friends struggling. However, we've been talking about the burnout crisis for years at this point, and nothing has been addressed on a systemic level. It keeps being thrust back on fundraisers as an individual problem. Unfortunately, because our mental and physical health are not prioritized by sector norms or leadership, it is up to us to take some steps to improve and preserve our well-being.

Because donor behavior is primarily prompted and inspired by the behavior of fundraisers, the sector's entire ecosystem depends on our ability to show up transparently, vulnerably, and authentically. Instead, we are operating from chronic stress, burnout, and constant dysregulation. This is an issue for every organization's bottom line and mission impact.

Previously, burnout was thought to only affect an individual's mental health, but now we know "the anxiety, depression, and sense of detachment that comes from burnout also spill over into people's intimate relationships. One of the reasons it does so is because burnout impacts our energy and energy is finite. Our ability to put energy into everything we do is a myth. When we work endless hours on campaigns, events, administrative, and marketing tasks, we often have no energy left to put into building and maintaining relationships" (McNichols 2021). Plus, it is difficult to empathize and attune to the emotional needs of others when we're emotionally exhausted and on edge.

When our nervous system is in a constant state of dysregulation or chronic stress, it becomes challenging to trust ourselves and others, be present in our interactions, or be open to change in a way that fosters growth and meaningful connection. When we can't form these connected relationships with donors, we are unable to move away from transactional fundraising, meaning we continue to prioritize behaviors that alleviate our immediate financial stress instead of taking actions that build long-term, healthy relationships. In chronic stress, fundraisers' nervous systems become a physical blockade to implementing sustainable fundraising practices. No matter how much fundraising advice we hear about the need to be authentic or vulnerable with our donors, when we're stressed, our body and nervous system are designed to prioritize survival. And as we now know, in that survival state, we do not have the mental, emotional, or physical capacity to truly engage. Yet we are doing very little to address the constant overwhelm that fundraisers are feeling, and instead continue to increase fundraising goals and add on urgency, pressure, judgment, and repercussions that exacerbate fundraiser stress, and the cycle continues.

We need to find ways to support fundraisers holistically, accounting for our energy levels and capacity. Preventative strategies and holistic support, like the frameworks we'll introduce in Part 2, are what enable us to create a new fundraising reality so we can raise more and feel good doing it. If leaders do not begin to comprehensively address the well-being of fundraisers, our capacity to fulfill the sector's expectations will be significantly compromised. I don't say this to foster or increase fundraiser feelings of victimhood or martyrdom. Quite the opposite—I want us all to understand this interconnection so that we can solve the right problems and each take accountability for our part of the equation.

By addressing both the psychological well-being of fundraisers and strategic fundraising practices in an integrated way, we can break free from transactional fundraising and build a sustainable approach that fosters genuine, authentic funder relationships and ultimately leads to greater fundraising success without the same risk of burnout.

Enter Alignment Fundraising.

PART II

The Solution

4 | Creating Inner Alignment

A few years ago, at my daughter's daycare, everyone was asked to gather in a circle and share what we did for work. I said I was a fundraiser, and I felt the eyes focus on me and quickly snap away. One grandfather even let out a full belly laugh, saying, "OK, well, don't ask me for money!"

It's natural that the first thing that comes to mind when we say the word *fundraising* is money because many people usually think about fundraising as just the financial transaction when money goes from a donor into a nonprofit. I like to think about it differently, though.

Fundraising is about inspiring people to contribute to something they care about. It has the power to encourage, help, and bring people together to invest in causes and communities in alignment with their values and the world they want to be a part of. When we connect individuals with a purpose that resonates with their values, incredible things happen. A single act of giving makes a genuine impact on the lives of others and on the givers themselves.

We, as fundraisers, know that it's about more than the money. Unfortunately, we're often trained or managed to focus only on the bottom line. When that is the underlying incentive for all of our communications, it's no wonder people like that grandfather make offhand comments or shy away from us. He assumed, like many do, that we'll take anyone's money and won't stop until we hear "yes." Although there are many sector-wide issues that led us here (as discussed at length in the previous chapters), as fundraisers, it's also time for us to do better: to work with passion and heart without making people feel like we only see their wallets when we approach them. To take accountability for our role in the system and shift our focus toward building real relationships rooted in partnership and mutual goals.

As we've discussed, even when we talk in our sector about building relationships, we're still primarily tracking the money. Despite what we say, our overwhelm and fear keep us tunnel-visioned so that we're still prioritizing how to meet and surpass a current funding goal. This money-first (and sometimes money-only) mindset leads to fundraising strategies that create the unfortunate conditions and results we are seeing in both the sector and in our experience as fundraisers.

The problems we're seeing throughout the sector are a result of tremendous misalignment.

When things are deeply out of alignment, fundraisers, organizations, and donors experience constant friction. We feel resistant in our fundraising, disingenuous in our communication, inauthentic in our leadership, and often trapped without choice in funder relationships or other power dynamics. This friction is palpable in everything from the tension during a donor meeting to a confusing donor giving experience on a website. These are all symptoms of misalignment.

What Is Alignment?

Alignment is function and action with ease. *Ease* is not a word we often hear in the nonprofit sector, but stay with me. There are ways in which we operate in the world that are filled with more flow and ease than others. When we prioritize alignment and, specifically, aligned partnerships with funders, we aren't constantly banging our heads against the wall. Instead, we're able to do our best work, creating more ease and flow in our partnerships, which leads to more success in our fundraising.

Alignment Fundraising happens when our communication, decision-making, and money movement all honor our core values and mission, while ethically sharing our assets with aligned partners and funders. Like authenticity, Alignment Fundraising involves being true to one's feelings, values, and beliefs, but it also requires empathy and an understanding of how to connect our core values and mission with those of potential funders. It prevents a lot of the discomfort and stress caused by transactional fundraising because of the way it helps us understand ourselves and the lens of our funders better so that we can easily identify where we are or aren't aligned. Partnership, mutual benefit, and finding a win-win opportunity are all cornerstones of Alignment Fundraising.

I am not the first person to talk about alignment when it comes to fundraising. However, part of Alignment Fundraising is learning how to consistently operate from an alignment-first mindset instead of falling back into money-first tendencies, particularly when forces like pressure, overwork, uncertainty, rejection, and isolation start to pull us toward chronic stress and burnout. This is why we start with inner alignment: to develop an understanding of the scarcity mindset, transactional fundraising, and the negative narratives that pull us out of alignment.

Alignment Fundraising starts with us and gives us clarity on how to move forward. When we can take a closer look at our attitude toward ourselves, money, and our ability to do our jobs well, we begin to see where these thoughts and beliefs contribute to the misaligned actions and outcomes that lead us toward burnout. When we have a clear understanding of what causes and contributes to our stress as fundraisers and how it affects our ability to access our true thoughts and feelings, we can better gauge our stress levels and intervene before it's too late. Learning about our internal dialogue and how it affects our outlook on every facet of our life, including fundraising, gives us the opportunity to create a new normal. When we can align our beliefs, energy, and thoughts with our goals and intended outcomes, we can focus on greater impact rather than just making it through the day.

Showing up this way creates the conditions for money movement: belonging, connection, and trusted relationships.

Unfortunately, over the years I've seen personal work dismissed on multiple occasions in favor of more fundraising strategies and templates. I vividly remember six months into my coaching practice, I was on the phone with a well-known fundraising consultant. We spoke about how much nonprofits were struggling with fundraising and debated the underlying cause.

"It's all about having the right strategy!" she exclaimed. "They just need to use the templates and materials we're giving them."

I shook my head. "But what if the biggest fundraising challenges aren't about the strategy or even the donor at all?" I asked. "What if we've been focused on the wrong thing all along and should be looking at fundraiser behavior instead of donor behavior? What if we need a new way of enabling fundraisers where we take care of the whole fundraiser—their discomfort and resistance—and give them the space to ground themselves, deal with rejection, and provide support through community? What if we need to deal with the stigma and limiting beliefs about fundraising once and for all?"

The consultant scoffed, and I could feel her eyes roll through the phone. "Everyone loves to talk about mindset, but that's not what I see. I have never even had a fundraiser tell me they are uncomfortable fundraising! What they all need is better time management and a better strategy." It was clear we weren't going to see eye-to-eye on this. We hung up at a stalemate, but our conversation stuck with me. In my opinion, there is an often-untapped tool kit to change our fundraising reality: executive coaching. These tools have the power to transform our fundraising to its core and enable us to reach our fullest potential.

Coaching to Overcome Fundraising Resistance

Distinct from consulting, mentorship, or facilitation, executive coaching's unique strength lies in clarifying and overcoming subconscious obstacles, such as limiting beliefs or self-doubt, that impede progress.

It brings clarity to the invisible, often subconscious, barriers that prevent us from taking action, making decisions, and ultimately reaching our goals. By addressing these barriers, people can function from a more empowered state, able to face challenges with flexibility, confidence, and courage.

Earning my certification as an iPEC Executive Coach wasn't a part of my fundraising plan at first. I became certified because I had always loved being coached and I enjoyed the coaching I was doing as a nonprofit leader. Although iPEC used much of the same vocabulary my personal coaches had used over the years, iPEC took my comprehension to a different level. I gravitated toward the way they used energy to gain a deeper awareness of what we're experiencing and as a tool to help make more conscious choices to achieve our goals. In my own life, I started to notice positive shifts in my experiences and results.

I knew I couldn't keep these tools all to myself. I began coaching women leaders from a variety of industries, including someone we'll call Ava, a mid-level insurance executive. Ava struggled with her confidence as a leader in a new role, specifically with managing staff, making critical decisions in public, and being open about mistakes with her team, which made her feel vulnerable and overwhelmed with doubt. Through our work together, she started to become conscious of the types of situations that would cause the most self-doubt and started to address her inner critic by creating space for her emotions, getting curious about her vulnerability, and ultimately offering new narratives that felt more empowering. The work she was doing internally affected the way she showed up as a leader—the clarity she had, the decisions she made, and the team she cultivated—which led to an increase in her success. And more confidence followed.

Ava's transformation inspired me to take a closer look at my career. I wondered where I was holding myself back, and if there were any common threads to my own challenges as a nonprofit leader. The answer was clear: asking for money made me feel vulnerable.

Fundraising itself brought up all of my limiting beliefs. It made me feel deeply uncomfortable, unworthy, and scared of not making everyone happy or doing something wrong. Once I began to lean on the iPEC principles and tools I used with my clients, I was able to see how my beliefs correlated with my results at work. Once I acknowledged and worked through the limiting beliefs that caused fear and resistance, I created a new level of success. A few weeks after integrating these tools and principles into my daily life, I was able to secure seven funder meetings: a staggering 87% return rate on my outreach efforts. This success translated into an influx of more than $450,000 in funding.

When we can recognize limiting beliefs and access these tools to overcome them, we're able to navigate situations with clarity and move through them in real time instead of coming to a halt. From this work, I understood two things: our internal dialogue directly affects our ability to take action, communicate clearly, build relationships, and show up as our best selves; and whom we're talking to is just as important as how we approach the conversation.

Raising money is deeply connected to our thoughts, beliefs, energy, and emotions toward talking about money. If those elements are rooted in scarcity, fear, and negativity, they block our ability to move more money into our organizations. It doesn't stop with mindset shifts, nor is it as simple as thinking positive. Once we release the insecurities about money itself, we have to align our actions in order to create the desired outcomes. This starts with understanding who your most aligned funders are and how to effectively invite them to get involved. Aligning our thoughts and actions gives us the opportunity to create sustainable strategies that work with us.

The Cognitive Loop

Several years ago, I addressed a group of high school students and their parents who were grappling with chemistry test anxiety. There was tangible tension in the air as I scanned the room. I took a moment, then said, "Chemistry is not stressful."

I watched their expressions change from stressed to confused to skeptical. I pressed on, explaining that the subject of chemistry itself wasn't inherently stressful. It was just a field of study, no different from others. Some students loved chemistry; some hated it.

The real stressor was the students' perceptions and beliefs about their capabilities in chemistry. Thoughts like "I'm bad at science," "I can't understand this content," "the teacher doesn't understand me," or "my brain just doesn't work this way" were the actual sources of their anxiety. The problem wasn't chemistry; it was their own internal narratives, their limiting beliefs, that heightened their stress, transforming an academic subject into a psychological hurdle.

The same hurdles apply to fundraising. Our internal narratives of our capabilities, fear of failure, money beliefs, and anxiety about others' perceptions of us influence how we feel about fundraising and ultimately the way we fundraise. This is why it is so important to identify when you're feeling discomfort fundraising and where that discomfort is coming from—is it rooted in your own fear or beliefs about money, value, or worth? Or is it because you've fallen for using a transactional fundraising norm that is never going to feel good to you or your donors? When things are vulnerable, like fundraising, and show up as feelings in our body, we need strategies that take that part of our experience into account if we want to get to the root cause of the challenges we're experiencing. Without a holistic approach like this, we fall into the decline discussed in Chapter 3: experiencing fundraising pressure, overwork, uncertainty, isolation, and rejection, which can escalate our discomfort into chronic stress and, ultimately, burnout.

Although the systemic issues in the sector and toxic workplaces stoke the stress of fundraising, there are also many underlying thoughts and beliefs inside us that exacerbate this tension. I started to understand this relationship through executive coaching and the cognitive loop. The *cognitive loop* is the idea that our beliefs inform our thoughts, our thoughts affect how we feel, and then, ultimately, how we feel influences how we show up, leading to our results and our reality (Figure 4.1). When these beliefs are rooted in stigmas, fear, or negative feelings, fundraising inevitably becomes a source of stress and a self-fulfilling prophecy. As I said before, we can only raise the amount of

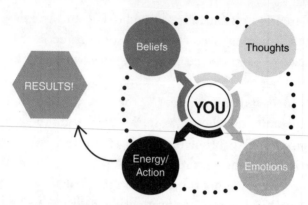

Figure 4.1 The cognitive loop.

money we believe is out there to be raised. Coaching and therapy practices have a few different ways of helping clients break unhelpful cycles through techniques that retrain the brain to believe a more positive or helpful thought.

Dr. Lisa Feldman Barrett, neuroscientist and author of more than 275 peer-reviewed papers and two books, *How Emotions Are Made* (2018) and *Seven and a Half Lessons on the Brain* (2020), talked about how the psychology of emotion helps us make sense of this connection. Barrett's revolutionary research has made her one of the top 0.1% most-cited scientists in the world because she helps us understand a fundamental part of being human: how our brains work. Her work sits at the intersection of neuroscience and psychology, offering life-changing insights about the role of emotions in our lives, why we feel what we do, and how we can harness the wisdom of our brains to feel better.

Barrett and I talked about how our brains work based on prediction and how we can train our brains to steer away from pain and anxiety and into a different present. Specifically, Barrett said, "Your brain is continuously using your past experience to anticipate the future, which becomes your present. And so, what this means is that emotions are not baked into your brain from birth. Your brain is making emotions on the fly as you need them" (Barrett 2021a).

Barrett's book *Seven and a Half Lessons About the Brain* gives an example of how exactly the predictive process works in the brain: "Think of the last time you were thirsty and drank a glass of water. Within seconds after draining the last drops, you probably felt less thirsty. This event might seem ordinary, but water actually takes about twenty minutes to reach your bloodstream. Water can't possibly quench your thirst in a few seconds. So, what relieved your thirst? Prediction. As your brain plans and executes the actions that allow you to drink and swallow, it simultaneously anticipates the sensory consequences of gulping water, causing you to feel less thirsty long before the water has any direct effect on your blood" (Barrett 2020, 71).

If we are used to past experiences that conjure up fear of fundraising, we can create a self-fulfilling prophecy for ourselves where we predict shortcomings and therefore conjure up self-sabotage anxiety into our present fundraising efforts. "So, what does your brain do when it can't predict very well? Well, certain chemicals become increased, and your heart beats faster, and you start to feel really jittery and worked up, and maybe even a bit more alert. But in our culture, the immediate go-to explanation of this is anxiety. . . . If your brain is making sense of an increase in arousal as anxiety, that will lead you to experience the arousal as negative and unpleasant. And also, it leads you to behave in a certain way" (Barrett 2021a).

Every instance of emotion is constructed from a combination of what is inside your brain (the remembered past) and the sensory present. When our brain makes predictions that construct anxiety, it can lead us to start to spiral downward. When we're expecting the worst, we can exacerbate our emotional strain so that we end up in chronic stress or burnout.

Part of the problem is, our predictions are not always accurate. We may be used to interpreting something in our heads as a threat (or being worthy of anxiety), when anxiety wasn't necessarily the appropriate response to begin with. In fact, Barrett said, "It's really important that people understand that every experience you have, every action you take, is caused partly by what's in your head and partly what's going on around you or inside you" (Barrett 2021a).

The good news is that our brains have the power to learn new pathways of prediction. Even as we experience discomfort, pressure, uncertainty, rejection, and so on, the brain can still learn new ways to react to these situations. And when it does, our behavior and results will change.

I spoke with Dr. Christian Busch, bestselling author of *The Serendipity Mindset* (2020), and an expert in the areas of innovation and purpose-driven leadership, about the role of mindset in success. Busch's research suggests the more we believe in the possibility of something, the more likely it is to happen. He found successful people have a unique ability to cultivate serendipity, rather than just wait for it. He reports that people with high degrees of success in their life "somehow see a little bit more in unexpected moments, and then they connect the dots and turn that into unexpected positive outcomes" (Busch 2023).

In the conversation, Busch shared research by fellow psychologist Dr. Richard Wiseman, author of *The Luck Factor: Change Your Luck, Change Your Life*, that demonstrated the power of our beliefs. Wiseman intentionally placed loose money and a fake businessman in a coffee shop before following two groups of people—one who self-identified as lucky and one who said they considered themselves stereotypically unlucky (Wiseman 2003). Importantly, neither group was necessarily luckier than the other; the groups were formed based on the individual's beliefs and perceptions about how lucky they were, but consistently, the research team found that people who self-identified as lucky were more likely to see the money, to talk to the businessperson, and to have an overall positive day, while those who self-identified as unlucky missed those opportunities. Each person had the opportunity to have serendipitous experiences. Whether or not this potential turned into reality was all in the power of belief.

Given the influence beliefs have on our lives, it's important we understand some of the primary beliefs fundraisers tend to have of themselves. In a 2023 anonymous survey, I asked fundraisers how they felt about their current experience as a fundraiser and my heart ached as I read through their responses:

- "Since I don't have much experience with fundraising, I won't be very good at it."
- "I'm not charming enough to be a fundraiser."
- "I don't have all the answers to questions that may be asked."
- "I am not good enough to successfully ask for [organization's] support."

These confessions remind me of exactly how I felt as a fundraiser for almost 13 years. What these fundraisers might not realize is just how much these beliefs affect their fundraising success. When I took a closer look at my beliefs about money, value, self-worth, and partnership I began to understand how those beliefs led to emotions that affected my ability to effectively fundraise. These negative beliefs were obstacles, creating resistance to taking critical actions in my fundraising. I used to think fundraising was always stressful, but I gradually understood that my perceptions and beliefs about money and fundraising were amplifying the stress more than the fundraising actions themselves. Now I understand that problems arise when we dismiss or stifle our emotions.

Our emotions about fundraising affect our approach and we can only address the emotions that we allow ourselves to have. As Barrett stated, "Your emotions critically influence your ability to connect. Fundraisers must pay attention to their brain and how they're feeling to be able to do their jobs with authenticity" (Barrett 2021a). Imagine the person who always surpasses their goals: the way they walk into a meeting with their head held high or jump into a virtual room radiating confidence. There's an air about them, almost as if they expect a great outcome. How do you think that person feels about fundraising? Do you think they would be able to have that energy if they were in chronic stress or burnout?

Recognizing the link between our thoughts, feelings, actions, and results is crucial—it is one way we prevent the decline from discomfort to burnout. The moment you begin to feel your feelings and dissect the root cause of those feelings is when you start to discover the ability to shift your mindset. It sparks a chain reaction that affects your energy, actions, and ultimately your outcomes.

Energy in Action

As fundraisers, we know that it's our job to create relationships with potential funders. All relationships have the potential to be authentic, positive, and mutually beneficial or fake, negative, and predatory. Think about how you feel after a great experience with a customer service representative who went the extra mile to help resolve your concerns versus walking out of a mall with a random bag of gadgets the guy at a kiosk talked you into buying. In the same way, some fundraising strategies feel aligned and harmonious, and some feel slimy and gross. This contrast underscores the crucial role of energy in aligning our practices with our core values and the right funders.

For years, I avoided using the word *energy* in my work out of fear it was too woo-woo and would dissuade people from using the framework, but it's more than a buzzword. Think about an empowering motivational speaker who resonates with an entire crowd, or a stressed-out leader whose presence causes a pit in your stomach. Their energy has a direct impact on those around them, and so does yours. In addition to how it affects the people around us, our energy determines if and how we take important fundraising actions in the first place.

When thinking about shifting your beliefs and approach to fundraising, you need to learn how to recognize the difference between *catabolic energy* and *anabolic energy*. According to Bruce D. Schneider, founder of iPEC and author of *Energy Leadership: The 7 Level Framework for Mastery in Life and Business*, "Anabolic energy is constructive, and catabolic energy is destructive" (Schneider 2022b, 263). Those who respond to a situation with "worry, fear, doubt, anger or guilt" (Schneider 2022b, 73) are experiencing catabolic energy. The more I studied the nervous system, the more I saw parallels with how catabolic energy was linked to our fight, flight, or freeze response to stress, fear, or anxiety. Think about how you react to something darting into the road while you're driving, an unexpected meeting request popping up on your calendar, or the dread you feel before a donor meeting. Sometimes, the catabolic or nervous energy can support you for a moment, but it can also keep you from showing up at your best, impairing your judgment or ability to approach a situation with clarity. When we rely on decisions rooted in catabolic energy, it will deplete us in the long run.

Prolonged periods of using catabolic energy can lead to chronic stress, disrupting our ability to fundraise. Here are some examples of how I believe catabolic energy shows up as stressful or anxiety-inducing experiences for fundraisers:

- **Fear of rejection.** The fear of rejection or not meeting expectations can contribute to the stress experienced before donor meetings. Thoughts like "they aren't going to like me" or "nothing ever goes my way in these meetings" indicate a catabolic response to the fear. Our fear also paralyzes us from taking a fundraising action that might lead to rejection (such as setting up other donor meetings), and the pressure mounts as the clock ticks down on our deadline.
- **Self-perception as a bad fundraiser.** Feeling uneasy or uncomfortable fundraising and choosing to believe these emotions make us bad at fundraising is another catabolic response that deters us from being able to focus and can intensify anxiety. Feelings of imposter syndrome, when we doubt our abilities and feel like we are not qualified for our role, can occur even with experienced fundraisers. This often leads to a state of over-drive, when we try to do all the things to feel busy, but the lack of focus means none of them move forward productively.

Different from catabolic energy, Schneider defines anabolic energy as constructive, expanding, fueling, healing, and growth-oriented energy typically rooted in joy, connection, and mutual benefit that helps move you forward with clarity and achieve positive, long-term results (Schneider 2022b). Using anabolic energy enables us to have a more complete and conscious view of what's happening and to come up with solutions and innovations more easily. If catabolic energy represents tunnel vision, anabolic energy helps us see a prism of opportunities.

We can apply the benefits of anabolic energy to our fundraising in many ways. We can notice the signals of anabolic energy, which can look like the following:

- **Flow state in a donor meeting.** In the midst of a key donor meeting, we find ourselves fully immersed in the conversation. Focused on the mutually beneficial opportunities between us and the donor, we passionately articulate our cause in ways that resonate deeply with the donor. Using anabolic energy gives us the opportunity to cocreate a visionary plan with funders.
- **Resilience in the face of challenges.** Operating from an anabolic state gives us the ability to make solution-focused decisions when challenges arise. When rejection happens, we understand it is a part of the process and recognize it was due to a lack of alignment rather than a personal failing. This shift enables us to approach donor meetings with curiosity and openness, rather than apprehension.

The 7 Levels of Energy

iPEC coaches use the Energy Leadership® Index assessment, which is a research-backed tool that measures your ability to lead yourself and others to take positive, productive, and sustainable action in your lives. I use this tool with my clients to help them understand their core beliefs, leadership styles, and to create a sustainable plan to approach their fundraising. Unlike other personality assessment tools (like the Enneagram and Myers Briggs), the Energy Leadership® Index is an attitudinal assessment.

The Energy Leadership® Index assessment categorizes a person's typical energetic makeup and their response to a stressful situation using seven energy levels, as explained in Schneider's *Energy Leadership* (Schneider 2022b). These levels help iPEC coaches and clients gain a better understanding of the energy they're bringing to their daily tasks, which then helps them form a strategy to shift into a more aligned response instead.

The levels correspond to a spectrum of catabolic to anabolic energy, with the lower levels (Levels 1–2) having the highest composition of catabolic energy, judgment, and tunnel vision. As the levels rise, so does the amount of anabolic energy. The highest levels (Levels 5–7) are where we tend to have more constructive, fueling, and expanding experiences. Figure 4.2 is an interpretation of each of Schneider's 7 Levels of Energy.

According to Schneider, there is no good or bad energy; on first read, it may seem that anabolic energy is "good" and catabolic energy is "bad," but he noted the good-bad juxtaposition is just another judgmental, binary way of thinking. Sometimes, the catabolic energy can protect us or point out a potentially harmful situation. The goal is to identify our energy level and then make a conscious choice about how we want to show up.

What's important to understand according to Schneider's *Energy Leadership* methodology is that we don't experience a singular energy level and stay there. We are consistently a combination of different energy levels, and we oscillate between them. Someone once helped me envision our experience of energy like the sound lights on an old boombox, flickering up and down as the song plays and with the beat of the music. We are always a combination of different levels, with one primary energy level during periods of calm and another primary energy level when we're in a stress response.

To gain a better understanding of the impact of energy on your thoughts and behaviors, here's a more detailed look at my interpretation of each of Schneider's 7 Levels of Energy.

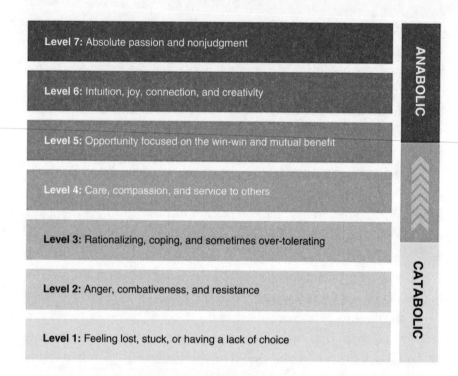

IT'S ALL ABOUT CONSCIOUS CHOICE.

Figure 4.2   Interpretation of each of Schneider's 7 Levels of Energy.

Source: Adapted from the Energetic Self-Perception chart, copyright Bruce D. Schneider 1999, 2006, 2022.

Energy Level 1: Victim

In *Energy Leadership*, Schneider describes Level 1 as having the highest concentration of catabolic energy; it's draining and can lead to feelings of powerlessness, feeling stuck, and feeling out of control. When we're in this state, we feel as though we have no choice, things are happening to us, and we aren't able to make them stop or move forward. We are essentially in self-preservation mode, avoiding everything, taking things personally, and overanalyzing.

My interpretation of how Level 1 shows up for fundraisers is that, at this level, we may experience victimhood or martyrdom and feel like we are not able to take any action or make decisions. To protect ourselves, we can go into people-pleasing or perfectionism. I've also seen fundraisers with a high amount of Level 1 energy oscillate between paralysis and hypervigilance, trying to stay as busy as possible but not completing anything or taking any vulnerable action. At this level of energy, we have little to no real engagement with others, and burnout could be around the corner.

Energy Level 1 in Practice

Leila has had a really tough year. Her last campaign didn't go as well as she had hoped, and she decided not to launch a new campaign because she was certain it would fail. Leila feels like she just keeps losing and letting her boss down, and when asked what she plans to do next to move forward, she rattles off a list of half-baked strategies that require a lot of her energy with little proof of return. She's constantly blaming her challenges on the lack of opportunities and donors—feeling like a victim of her circumstances. She clocks 60+-hour weeks and still isn't able to bring in any new funding, and she has resigned herself to believe there isn't anything else she can do.

Energy Level 2: Antagonist

Level 2 brings a mindset of anger, defiance, and conflict (Schneider 2022b). It's more action oriented than Level 1, but is often driven by a desire to fight against circumstances rather than work with them. According to Schneider, whereas Level 1's philosophy might be "I lose," the outlook of a Level 2 energy is "you lose." At this energy level, we are more likely to become angry and lash out, or find it difficult to let things go. Level 2 judgment is frequently binary, and there is a tendency to blame others when something goes awry. When we are in a Level 2 energy, I believe we might feel anger that funders aren't giving us as much as we want or expect, for example, or we might feel angry at other organizations we perceive as competition or cannibalizing funding.

Energy Level 2 in Practice

Mei-Ling has reached a point of sheer frustration. She's a fundraiser at a small health care nonprofit and feels like she can't get the time of day from funders who are more interested in large nonprofits. She constantly says, "I can't believe they are giving to that organization instead of us." Although she has been cranking out outreach emails, she is still struggling to meet her funding goals, and blames the competing nonprofits for taking opportunities she feels entitled to because her organization "needs it more than they do." This energy comes through when she meets with donors, and they tend to walk away feeling taken for granted.

Energy Level 3: Rationalizer

At Level 3, individuals are better able to cope with challenges through rationalization and tolerance (Schneider 2022b). This level is about finding ways to adapt and work within constraints, though it can also involve passively allowing toxic environments or uncomfortable situations in an attempt to maintain peace, and issues with self-blame can remain quite prevalent.

When we apply Level 3 to fundraising, I see us beginning to move forward with tasks like outreach to prospective funders, but in a somewhat lackluster and status quo way. We might hear ourselves say, "it's fine," or "that's just the way it is," essentially resigning as opposed to taking action in an empowered and excited manner. This energy level can also include delay tactics that hinder our forward motion. These ever-moving goalposts aren't about actually being ready; they are about protecting ourselves from the vulnerability of reaching out and asking for support or partnership.

Energy Level 3 in Practice

Jamal has been making progress with his end-of-year fundraising campaign, but has hit a few roadblocks lately. His mantra is "it's fine," which helps him cope with disappointments, but it doesn't get him excited about the work. He's happy to get a meeting with a long-term donor, but he doesn't ask for what he really needs and doesn't feel empowered to respectfully negotiate when they suggest restricting their funding. Jamal blames himself for undervaluing the work and not having a more transparent conversation about restricted funding, but rationalizes that if he had asked for more or pushed back it could have led to the donor refusing to give anything at all.

Energy Level 4: Helper

According to Schneider, Level 4 is characterized by a focus on helping others, compassion, and service. It's about putting the needs of others first, which sometimes means not enforcing our own boundaries. "People who function at Level 4 tend to have lots of sympathy and a pronounced need to 'fix' other people. At this level, you can feel frustrated or drained if you're unable to help someone get 'better'" (Schneider 2022b).

In my experience, this level is incredibly common for fundraisers. After all, what brings so many of us into this sector is a deep care for others and a desire to help. This can be valuable for fostering relationships and collaboration with funders. We want our funders to achieve their aligned goals through a partnership and to make sure they feel good about their investment. But sometimes, we're willing to make our funders happy at all costs, which can over-center the donor and maintain problematic power dynamics.

I've seen many people in Level 4 energy suffer from compassion or service fatigue when we take on the stress and trauma of others, which can affect our ability to exercise empathy and connect with other people in the long run (Clay 2022). At this level, we might also fall into the trap of helping more from a desire to be liked than to be effective.

Energy Level 4 in Practice

Sunita has always considered herself a helper. She exudes compassion and empathy, and she looks for ways she can lift up others. She's highly skilled at tuning into the needs of funders and is great at finding opportunities for collaboration, but often finds herself putting the needs of the funder above her own. When a funder emails her about a small issue, she thinks, "I need to email them back now, and fix this right away or else they won't keep working with us." Although she has a lot of fundraising success because of her energy, sometimes it leads her to a state of complete exhaustion where she is no longer able to connect and becomes frustrated with herself and resentful of her situation, dropping her from Level 4 to Level 1 or 2.

Energy Level 5: Collaborator

Schneider notes that Level 5 is even more grounded in anabolic energy. This level is adept at finding mutually beneficial, win–win opportunities. We see potential in everything and everyone, and we stop believing everything must be fixed. When fundraisers operate at this level, we genuinely believe in our ability to achieve both the funder's goals and the goals of the community and organization. In my experience, Level 5 is often the difference between a simple sponsorship (where one partner helps the other) and a strategic partnership (where both parties mutually benefit). At this level of fundraising, we're likely to generate new ideas, be more productive, and be better equipped to recognize a no as an opportunity to refocus on aligned partnerships.

Energy Level 5 in Practice

Blake sees possibilities in everything. Each time they talk to a potential donor, they look for win-win opportunities that benefit not only their organization and the communities they serve but also offer unique assets to the funder. When they get a no, they respect it and see it as an opportunity to learn and find new partnerships more in alignment. When Blake sees a gap their organization could fill, they say to themself, "I think there is something our organization can really help with here. I wonder what's possible and if our donors can cocreate that with us."

Energy Level 6: Connector

According to Schneider, Level 6 is characterized by a deep sense of interconnectedness and joy. When we're experiencing Level 6 energy we have a more holistic view of situations and trust our intuition when making decisions; this is often the level of energy that describes visionary leaders as well. We might be experiencing Level 6 energy when we sit down to work and get so excited by what we're doing we completely lose track of time.

When we're experiencing a lot of Level 6, we can quickly sense when we are not in alignment with a potential funder and know how to respectfully walk away. The key advantages of this level include a high capacity for staying mindful, calm, and present, and an acumen for inspiring greatness in others. However, when we're at this level of anabolic energy, it is possible we might come off as ungrounded, especially because it might be hard to articulate our vision to others who are not in the same state.

Energy Level 6 in Practice

Sofia is truly excited when she shows up to work. She sees each conversation with a funder as an opportunity to deepen an authentic connection. She's incredibly intuitive and able to identify alignment quickly, making her fundraising effective and efficient. Her colleagues remark on her wisdom and ability to stay joyful and creative, even as the end-of-year deadlines loom. When they ask her how she stays so centered, Sofia says, "This is an incredible opportunity for us to come together and look at the big picture."

Energy Level 7: Creator

Schneider's highest energy level, Level 7, embodies a state of absolute fearlessness and nonjudgment. Although no one lives primarily at this level of energy, it is possible to have bursts of Level 7 energy throughout our day. Energy Level 7 can't be shown in practice the same way as the other levels because, as Schneider explains, "at Level 7, the three-dimensional world that you think you know and see becomes obscure and indefinable"(Schneider 2022b, 198).

Fundraisers accessing this level of energy have "access to truth beyond illusion" and "absolute passion," (Schneider 2022b, 198), which allows us to experience moments of fearlessness and consciously create our world. Schneider reminds us that "Level 7 is an energy that cannot be sustained; it can only be tapped into from time to time" (Schneider 2022b, 198), but even those moments, though hard to describe, can be incredibly helpful for fundraisers when we need to take a risk in our fundraising strategy, start a difficult conversation with a funder, or take on a challenge.

Case Study: Liberty Franks

Learning to Harness Her Energy and Say No

"I'm so sorry," Liberty Franks said, almost as much to herself as to her former employer, the CEO of a multimillion-dollar non-profit. "I can't do this anymore."

Although Liberty cared about the work she was doing, and she liked her colleagues, she still felt completely and utterly alone, constantly stressed, and desperate for relief. She was ready to leave the sector all together when she logged on to watch one of my webinars.

During this particular webinar, I explained the impact of catabolic and anabolic energy to fundraisers and sector leaders, helping them understand how important it is to have access to higher levels of energy in order to make progress. I shared stories about why tapping into catabolic energy makes us more susceptible to feelings of victimhood and of binary thinking, which leads us to think if someone doesn't respond to our email, then it's the end of the world.

I explained that once we're able to shift our energy level and operate from more anabolic energy, we start to see more opportunities. We can take a breath. In that state of being, someone not responding to our email feels less catastrophic—they might be busy and it's worthy of a follow-up.

Liberty had a profound realization once she learned about the different styles of energy. "It's not that I wanted to leave fundraising," she said in a follow-up conversation. "I wanted to leave the way I felt."

Liberty was a perfect example of the rollercoaster of emotions I refer to as the 4-1-3 cycle. The Level 4 helper energy drove her desire to serve and provide solutions, but the lack of personal boundaries led to the depletion of her own energy.

(continued)

(*continued*)

When we're not aware of our energy, our helpfulness can very quickly devolve into martyrdom when we experience an instance of disrespect, rejection, or resistance. We've gone from Level 4 to Level 1, and suddenly it all becomes too much to bear. We freeze and begin to overanalyze every piece of our approach, falling into a perfectionism that keeps us from any progress.

Then, we start to rationalize whatever sent us to Level 1 with excuses. This is Energy Level 3 rationalization, when we think, "This is a really crazy time. They probably don't have time to meet with me anyway. I'll just follow up again in 30 days." After that, we slowly make our way back to Level 4.

But then the cycle will inevitably repeat.

Reflecting, Liberty said, "When I was in Level 1 energy, it was so easy for me to descend to a place of scarcity, of reactionary fundraising, of overwhelm, instead of staying in my superpower place where I was really connecting with people."

The superpower place Liberty references are Levels 5 through 7. This is where we are rooted in mutual benefit, joy, and connection, and even experience fearlessness at Level 7.

She shared a beautiful reflection on her energy journey: "We're whole people coming to fundraising. Just like there are seasons of our life, there are seasons of energy. It's all about choosing where you're going next."

Once Liberty understood how her thoughts, beliefs, and energy levels were intertwined, she started to manage the experiences that previously put her into a state of overwhelm and shift her energy in the moment. With this newfound power, Liberty realized she wasn't ready to give up on fundraising.

"I came full circle. Instead of saying that I wanted to leave this sector, I was able to get to a place in my body where I felt safe and in control. I was able to say that I need to keep doing this work. There's a place [in fundraising] for me."

Like Liberty, once we are aware of our energy levels, we can begin to address the barriers creating resistance in our fundraising and holding us back from building real relationships with donors. We need to be able to choose anabolic energy and shift into it in the moment so we don't stay stuck in low energy cycles. Once we're operating from higher levels of anabolic energy, we are more open to connection and can build mutually beneficial and aligned partnerships rooted in the level of transparency and authenticity we desire.

Increasing Your Anabolic Energy

As I learned from Schneider's work, bringing awareness to your beliefs, thoughts, actions, and the circumstances that activate your catabolic energy is a critical prevention strategy to avoid the decline from discomfort to burnout. This self-awareness is not about creating an unrealistic view that everything is possible if you just believe. It's about understanding how our internal dialogue can either move us forward or hold us back by activating the chronic stress that inhibits action and creates a barrier to authentic relationship building.

It's essential to strike a balance in taking accountability for the challenges we face without ignoring the inequity of challenges presented. Not all obstacles are within our own minds, and external systemic issues and toxic workplaces play a meaningful role in the fundraising results we see across the sector. No amount of internal work can replace the need for systems level change. Shifting our energy does not discredit or downplay the serious inequities faced in our society either. At the same time, the more we recognize where we do have control over how we show up, the larger impact we can have on these systemic issues. If we have more capacity to participate from a place of conscious choice, to see clearly what needs to change and how, we will be able to create and contribute to more effective solutions.

The nonprofit sector, like many others, is fraught with systemic issues that require collective action and change. These are not mere perceptions but are material realities that affect our daily work. We may not be able to reduce the number of situations that will cause us stress but we can address what happens when we do get activated by gaining insight into the Big Four Energy Blocks as described by Schneider in *Energy Leadership* (2022b)—limiting beliefs, interpretations, assumptions, and the gremlin—and by having tools to quiet the internal negative dialogue associated with them.

Limiting Beliefs

Limiting beliefs are deeply held convictions that constrain us in some way, diminishing our ability to achieve our personal and professional goals (Schneider 2022b). They might include thoughts like "I can't ask for more money; they'll say no" or "Our organization isn't big enough to attract large donations." These beliefs halt the potential of what nonprofits can achieve because they cap the actions we take and the strategies we employ in our daily work. Limiting beliefs are rarely rooted in objective data, but they can become self-fulfilling prophecies if we allow them to influence our behavior.

Running a four-minute mile is hard, but we know it's possible. That wasn't always the case. Until the mid-1950s, running a four-minute mile was thought to be unachievable, something that would push the human body to the absolute limit of its physical capabilities. Turns out, it wasn't the body creating the barrier—it was the mind. In 1954, Roger Bannister shattered this belief when he ran a mile in 3 minutes and 59 seconds, an incredible record-breaking feat (Schneider 2022b, 130–131).

Bannister's story can teach us about commitment and unwavering perseverance in the face of doubt, but what I find most fascinating is what happened afterward. Just 46 days later, John Landy broke Bannister's record, managing to complete a mile in just 3 minutes and 58 seconds (Schneider 2022b). Once Bannister showed others it was possible to do this, the mental barriers holding back other runners fell.

Without these limiting beliefs, they were able to achieve unthinkable milestones. This is why it's so important to recognize and start to shift the limiting beliefs we hold in fundraising.

To help you uncover limiting beliefs you might be holding, consider the following questions:

- What do I believe is possible for my organization? Are there beliefs that limit what I think we can achieve?
- What narratives do I tell myself about my ability to succeed in fundraising?
- Am I holding onto beliefs about the "right way" to fundraise that might be limiting me?

Interpretations

According to Schneider, *interpretations* are opinions or judgments that we create about an event, situation, person, or experience. For example, we can interpret a lack of reply to an email as the potential donor being mad at us or if a funder cancels our meeting at the last minute, we interpret it as them not wanting to be involved in our organization anymore.

The key here is that we believe these things to be true, and create entire narratives around them, even if they're not actually based in reality. That potential donor might have missed our email in the deluge of messages they get each day. Their behavior may have absolutely nothing to do with their commitment to our organization.

But because we treat our interpretations as facts, we can easily miss these likely possibilities and become stuck in our negative thoughts. Through the cognitive loop, these interpretations can become reality because we ultimately behave in a way that creates a self-fulfilling prophecy.

Consider these questions when determining how you interpret fundraising scenarios:

- When a funder doesn't respond to my outreach, how do I perceive their behavior?

- When a donor doesn't support a certain initiative, what do I think is the reason for their behavior?
- When a donor makes a suggestion to our organization, what conclusions do I draw about their opinion of us?

Assumptions

Schneider defines an *assumption* as an expectation that because something has happened in the past, it will happen again. Assumptions can be positive or negative. In fundraising, for example, we may believe someone will want to increase their donation after attending an inspiring and successful event in the past. Or, conversely, we may believe someone doesn't want to support our organization's upcoming GivingTuesday event because they declined in the past, or we assume because we were rejected from a foundation in the past we shouldn't apply for their current grant cycle.

Negative assumptions are often based on fear. When I ask fundraisers why they don't want to ask a funder who said no last year to sponsor their gala this year, they often realize it's because they're afraid of rejection. But this time, we might get a yes, and no matter what, we don't want to be making decisions on behalf of our donors without even giving them the opportunity to participate.

I'm all about using data to inform our decisions, but we have to make sure we're not pulling on data that's rooted in fear, or forgetting to apply new data that would change the circumstance (such as the donor has a new job, is in alignment with a new program, or became a volunteer over the last year).

When you're making decisions about your donors and fundraising activities, here are a few questions to ask to catch any assumptions you might be making:

- What common assumptions do I make about donors who haven't given in a year?
- Just because x situation was true before, does it have to be true again? Why or why not?

- What steps can I take to ensure I'm not making decisions *for* donors, but rather providing them with opportunities to make informed choices?

Gremlins

According to Schneider, the fourth energy block is the *gremlin*—the voice in our head that tells us not to try, to avoid risks at all costs, and to compromise our life by telling us to play it safe and stay small. The gremlin thrives on fear, and when we hear the voice it leads to dread and fear of failure. It's different from the self-critic that beats us up about past events; instead, it focuses on sabotaging future actions. (Schneider 2022b, 143) Often, we hear our gremlin voice in messages of "not enoughness." When it comes to fundraising, I often have fundraisers share that they hear a relentless voice telling them that they don't know enough, aren't experienced enough, outgoing enough, or well-liked enough to be a good fundraiser.

Addressing the gremlin is highly personal, but the very first step is to acknowledge the gremlin's existence. In *Energy Leadership*, Schneider offers a helpful way to bring awareness to our gremlin by giving it a name, which helps separate the gremlin from our true selves.

To help us build awareness around our own gremlin voice as it relates to fundraising, here are some questions to consider:

- What internal voices or thoughts do I hear when I think about taking risks or stepping outside my comfort zone in fundraising? How do these voices influence my decision-making process in fundraising situations?
- When do I notice these voices the most? Is it during donor interactions, when inviting people to contribute, when planning fundraising events, or at other times?
- How might my fundraising efforts change if I were able to diminish the influence of this gremlin voice?

If you have experienced one of Schneider's Big Four Energy Blocks or countless other negative thoughts fundraisers hold, know that you are not alone. These thought patterns are incredibly prevalent and are reinforced by broader forces in the nonprofit sector. Just beginning to notice the thoughts and narratives, instead of accepting them as facts, will start to shift how you feel and ultimately how you show up.

I don't want to be reductive, though, because mindset work is hard and sometimes remembering to ask ourselves a reframing question is far easier said than done. Common limiting beliefs, interpretations, and assumptions can lead to debilitating thoughts like "I can't do this" and activate our feelings of overwhelm. So, if we're entering a spiral where the negative narrative in our head is creating these feelings and emotions, sometimes we need a quicker remedy to address it effectively.

Strategies to Stop the Spiral

In moments when we feel like the negative thoughts and catabolic energy are taking over, I've found it helpful to turn to a set of strategies to help calm my thoughts.

Strategy 1: Embracing Discomfort Discomfort can show up for a lot of different reasons, but trying to embrace and reframe it (when appropriate, as discussed in Chapter 3) can either quickly shift our energy or provide us with clarity about why we're feeling that discomfort in the first place.

When you notice discomfort, take a moment to sit with it:

- Notice that you feel something.
- Notice that it's uncomfortable.
- You will resist it (this is normal).
- Notice your resistance to it.
- Welcome the resistance. Sometimes I say, "Oh, hi there, you're welcome here."

If your body relaxes, witness the sensations as you create space for the discomfort and watch the feeling pass. Celebrate the fact that you had awareness of the discomfort in the first place.

If you feel stuck in the resistance, even when you give it space, start to explore where that resistance is coming from. Sometimes I'll ask myself, "What am I afraid of right now?" Usually, a certain fear will jump to the surface. Here, we can invite a reframe. For example, I might say to myself, "Discomfort is a great sign. It means I am exactly where I should be, doing exactly what I need to be doing. This is how I grow." Then pause to reflect and see how that starts to make you feel.

Embracing this type of discomfort isn't just about tolerating it; it's about recognizing its value as a catalyst for growth and impact. That is why it's so important to celebrate these moments of discomfort as clear signs that you are moving forward and growing, not just in fundraising but also in your personal development and leadership. You should note, in the event that none of these strategies work, it might be time to consider that this is a different type of discomfort coming from a harmful environment, misalignment, or transactional fundraising practices that need to be examined and addressed.

Strategy 2: Acknowledge and Validate   Although it's clear that being overwhelmed as a fundraiser is not unique, we still feel the need to push away our feelings and persevere. In my 2023 survey, 79% of fundraisers try to push away their feelings when they're experiencing dysregulation. Although it might seem like putting our head down and powering through is the best way, attempting to ignore what we are feeling only exacerbates the situation. As I've mentioned previously, we can only manage the emotions we allow ourselves to have. Emotional avoidance is not the same thing as a positive mindset. Particularly important for fundraising, there is evidence that shoving aside emotions inhibits your ability to make social connections (Srivastava et al. 2014).

Drawing on the research, Britt Frank said, "When we gaslight ourselves out of reality, we end up creating more of the thing that we're trying to get out of. If you don't acknowledge that your leg is broken and you keep trying to walk on it, you can say all the positive affirmations you want, but that leg is going to become more and more problematic. And then we're going to have a real crisis on our hands" (Frank 2022b).

Frank offers a simple strategy that has been revolutionary for me and many fundraisers I have coached. Recognizing that "a self-validation moment is almost always a faster way out of the thing you're dealing with than trying to pretend it doesn't exist," her first step is to recognize the thoughts and the feelings you're having. Once you're aware of a negative thought or a feeling of fear deep in your belly, say to yourself "it makes sense" (Frank 2022b). For example:

- It makes sense that I'm afraid of putting that proposal in front of the donor. I'm worried they might say no, and I know rejection can hurt.
- It makes sense that I'm nervous about this donor meeting. I didn't hear back from the last donor I met with and being ghosted made me question whether I had done something wrong.
- It makes sense that I feel anxious about sending out that first fundraising campaign email. We've worked so hard and I am afraid it won't have the response I'm hoping for.

It is amazing the speed at which this sentence can change your experience. Frank describes it as "if your brain is on fire, the phrase 'it makes sense' is like taking a nice little bucket of water and putting it out" (Frank 2022b).

Although this strategy might sound simple, it will take practice. Giving ourselves space to understand and validate our emotions can help us become better equipped to navigate the complex landscape of fundraising, which can ultimately lead to more connected relationships with donors.

Strategy 3: Distanced Self-Talk   I read *Chatter: The Voice in Our Head, Why It Matters, and How to Harness It* by Dr. Ethan Kross (2021a) in 24 hours, and it was what inspired me to start my podcast. Kross is a psychologist and neuroscientist who has pioneered research in how people talk to themselves and the ways the voice in our head affect every facet of our day-to-day lives.

Dr. Kross defines *chatter* as the negative dark side of the inner voice (Kross 2021a). Kross said that experiencing chatter is completely normal and common, but it can also be debilitating. Although there are many strategies to address chatter, one of my favorites is called *distanced self-talk*. Kross describes this as "using your name and the second person pronoun 'you' to coach yourself through a problem" (Kross 2021a).

Imagine you're about to walk into a high-stakes donor meeting. The chatter in your head might sound something like "I'm so nervous. I can't mess this up like last time. If I don't get this right, I'm not going to be able to hit my funding goal for the year and we won't be able to launch our new program." Using language that mimics us talking to someone else, we can gain perspective and are better equipped to speak to ourselves with the same compassion and objectivity we would offer a good friend. So, instead, I might say, "Mallory, you know you're aligned with this funder. You've done the prep work. You can do this."

It might feel odd at first, but this reframing isn't just about positive thinking. It's about pulling ourselves out of tunnel vision. Distanced self-talk works by "leverag[ing] the structure of language . . . allowing [us] to seamlessly adopt the perspective of a distanced observer" (Orvell et al. 2021).

Strategy 4: Curiosity over Judgment For many years, a sticky note sat on the bottom of my computer that simply said "get curious." It was such a small reminder, but I found seeing it out of the corner of my eye while drafting my third follow-up email to a potential donor helped shift me out of the judgment that so often plagued my past fundraising. Getting stuck in self-doubt and judgment are characteristics of the lower levels of catabolic energy and can lead to the chronic stress and burnout that disconnect us from people and sabotage authentic relationship building. Judgment is important—it can help us think critically and solve complex problems, but it can also be highly problematic when judgment starts to occur at the expense of curiosity (by showing up as limiting beliefs, interpretations, or assumptions).

Studies show there are many benefits to curiosity—including fewer decision-making errors, more innovation, reduced conflict, more transparent communication, and better team performance—that we might miss out on if we choose to jump straight to judgment (Gino 2018).

Judgment of ourselves and judgment of our funders create resistance and tunnel vision; curiosity creates a spectrum of opportunity. The two go hand in hand. We cannot reduce judgment in one area and not the other. If we try to get curious about the behavior of a funder in order to show compassion, but fall right back into judgment of ourselves when we don't behave perfectly, we'll wind up back in catabolic energy with resistance, and the cycle continues. This is why a common first step to breaking a chronic stress response is self-compassion.

Here are strategies I've found helpful when I've been stuck in judgment and need a way to increase my curiosity:

- **Embrace awareness.** Similar to the advice to acknowledge and validate your feelings, simply taking a minute to recognize a moment of judgment can be helpful. Try to get curious about what you might be judging and why. Is it something that serves you? If not, what reframe might be available to you? You can also ask yourself, what would I say to a friend right now?
- **Get comfortable with open-ended questions.** When it comes to curiosity of self, you might ask open-ended questions such as: what are my motivations here? What might I be afraid of? Regarding judgment of others, you might ask, how can I show compassion or understanding instead of making this judgment and assumption?
- **Write down the exact opposite story.** When I have a client committed to the story in their head and they are struggling to explore other truths or options, I ask them to write down their narrative on one side of the paper, flip it over, and then write the exact opposite story. This helps open a window of curiosity

about what other truths might be possible and what it would feel like to embody a different narrative.

Once we understand the important role of energy; identify the limiting beliefs, interpretations, assumptions, and gremlin narratives that may be holding us back; and have the tools we need to address our negative thought patterns, we become more connected and in alignment with ourselves. This enables us to engage in effective fundraising that feels good. In addition to the tools we've reviewed to address energy and looping thoughts, somatic and embodiment practices have also been important in my own journey. I'm not going to expand on them more in this book, other than to endorse their important role in holistically supporting the wellness of fundraisers. Anything that supports awareness in our brain and body and moves us toward a more positive relationship with ourselves will help us fundraise in a way that is rooted in anabolic energy and mutually beneficial partnerships. The lessons in this chapter not only address what's happening inside of us, but they enable us to put Alignment Fundraising into practice.

5

Alignment Fundraising Strategy

For nearly 13 years, I fundraised in a completely scattered way, basically throwing spaghetti at the wall, praying something would stick so that we would meet our annual fundraising goal. As the managing director of a nonprofit that had just passed the million-dollar mark, I was determined to expand our reach. Through excessive effort and primarily through diversified corporate sponsorships, our revenue grew to $1.7 million. Despite this success, we were still not getting a lot of funding from foundations. The board incessantly pressured me to increase these funds.

One afternoon, overwhelmed by my task list and bracing for an upcoming board meeting, a realization dawned on me. We were not aligned with most foundations. Our priorities, business model, and program designs were vastly different from what foundations in our issue area were seeking. This awareness marked the beginning of my understanding that Alignment Fundraising was a different methodology from what most organizations were practicing. I saw how essential it was to recognize and embrace our organization's identity, and to find funders who shared our core beliefs and goals, and who appreciated the value our organization brought to the community and our partnership.

From this perspective, it was clear that foundation funding—which in this particular instance primarily focused on scientific research—did not align with our organization's long-term goals or vision to provide virtual ungated education to the masses.

I prepared a detailed presentation for the board, highlighting our misalignment and emphasizing the importance of aligning values, mission, goals, assets, and program tactics with funders. It wasn't just about not meeting the funder's criteria for research outcomes; these foundations weren't the partners we needed to scale our education programs.

I'm happy to say that the board heard me out. Even the most skeptical members recognized the importance of aligning with the right funders and how this could optimize our fundraising efforts. With their support, I fully embraced Alignment Fundraising methods. I started to receive corporate funds with fewer strings attached, enabling me to be more direct with funders and showcase the value sponsorship of our educational resource provided to funders beyond the program's goals—including networking, brand association, audience engagement, and cause marketing opportunities. This shift brought authenticity to my approach, reducing resistance and anxiety about fundraising. And before I knew it, our organization crossed the $3 million mark.

As I aligned more with our mission, values, and unique organizational assets, funders responded positively. The synergy brought tangible progress toward our cause, making the collaboration feel good to everyone involved. I stopped waiting for responses from uninterested parties and started attracting *Power Partners*: individuals, foundations, or corporations open to creating mutually beneficial strategic partnerships with nonprofits; or nonprofit leaders who show up with vulnerability, assets, and courage to build mutually beneficial partnerships with funders.

Building Power Partnerships led me to decline funding that didn't align and provided a reprieve from self-doubt spirals. Rejections clarified unaligned potential partners, which changed the power dynamics between me and the funders. Fundraising was no longer about hounding people for money, but understanding our mutual values and shared goals.

Alignment Fundraising became more than a strategy; it was a mindset that transformed fundraising from a transactional, dreaded task to a collaborative, empowering process. This approach improved our finances and enabled us to foster a thriving community of funders based on authenticity, trust, and shared commitment to our cause.

The Layers of Alignment Fundraising

Once I saw how implementing Alignment Fundraising strategies improved my work, I was curious. I dug deeper to identify the different facets of alignment I was starting to experience with funders. I noticed there were some similarities among my new Power Partners. We aligned in three or more of the following ways:

- **Value alignment.** Funders who resonate with our core values, beyond mere agreement on paper. Once we understand our organization's values, we can better identify which partners share those values and will demonstrate them throughout the partnership.
- **Mission alignment.** Partners with a shared vision and mission, ensuring we're working toward the same goals. We don't have to share all of the same incentives for goals, but we need to have a shared North Star.
- **Tactical/strategic alignment.** It's one thing to want the same outcome, but it's another to believe in the same program, structure, or methods to achieve it. Tactical and strategic alignment means collaborating with those who trust and value our methods and strategies in realizing our shared mission.
- **Tracking and reporting alignment.** Aligning on success metrics, ensuring both parties value and understand each other's indicators of success and are looking to track many of the same things. If funders and organizations are misaligned on

metrics of success—where one partner is looking at indicators for breadth of impact (e.g., number of students served) while the other is looking at indicators that demonstrate depth of impact (e.g., number of hours each student spends in the program)—it can lead to a lot of friction in translating impact and can often lead to mission drift for the organization.

- **Asset alignment.** Assets are all of the things of value inside of our organization. When a nonprofit has assets a funder is interested in, there is asset alignment. For example, a corporation may value a nonprofit's social media reach and want to incorporate cause marketing into the partnership to increase their visibility. We expand on how to find and leverage assets later in this chapter.

Ensuring these layers of alignment with funders helps fundraisers move away from the transactional mindset of "you have money; we need money" toward creating transformative, win–win partnerships that thrive on mutual growth and success. This approach fosters alignment in resources, visions, strategies, and values. Fundraising becomes about building partnerships that are ethical, empathetic, and deeply connected to our core mission and values.

Many have done this with the Power Partners Formula™. And although the formula has catalyzed a lot of incredible financial wins over the years, one of the best days was when a client turned down $1 million because it was out of alignment with their organization's focus and would have required staff and support the organization did not have. They realized that a seven-figure check would actually cost them more than it was worth in the long run and cause mission drift. The organization understood that money is not the only thing of value and that alignment is much more important. Instead, they opted to receive a $120,000 donation from the same funder to support a project that directly affected their current goals. The next year, the funder made an additional $185,000 investment.

To feel differently as fundraisers, we need to fundraise differently. To fundraise differently, we need to think differently about how we fundraise and be open to real partnerships.

Case Study: Hilary Wolkan

How an Alignment-First Approach Transformed Her Fundraising and Mental Health

I first met Hilary Wolkan when she was an individual giving manager for the Institute for Sustainable Communities, a global nonprofit that works to advance climate justice and support frontline communities facing the brunt of the climate crisis. She decided to join the Power Partners Formula™ to boost her skills.

"I had been finding that the traditional way of trying to widen our donor pool was really not working the way I wanted it to," she said. "I was going up to everyone, shaking them and saying 'give us money, give us money, give us money.' It didn't matter who they were or if they even cared about the work I did." Unsurprisingly, Hilary was getting a *ton* of rejections using a money-first approach. "It was exhausting and terrifying, and we were getting lots and lots and lots of 'nos.'"

Once she dove deeper into the Power Partners Formula™ and began receiving support, Hilary set up a meeting and had a wonderful conversation with a potential donor. She came to the meeting with authenticity, transparency, and belief in herself as a fundraiser. She spoke unapologetically about the programs she hoped to fund. Turns out, the donor wasn't really looking to have a corporate philanthropy program. So even though they were mission-aligned, they weren't a good funding fit.

However, because Hilary approached the conversation with confidence, the potential donor offered to introduce her to his wife, who worked for a donor-advised fund and had a client

(continued)

(*continued*)

looking to support exactly what Hilary's nonprofit did. It was a match made in alignment.

By being open to receiving a no, Hilary got the yes.

By shifting her focus to aligned partners, she increased her funding, decreased her resistance, and stopped adding more work to her plate by accepting the wrong money. She found her Power Partners.

Hilary also said this work greatly decreased her anxiety. Before working with me, when she inevitably received a rejection, she felt horrible. She took everything personally and felt like she was failing herself and her organization.

When a donor ghosted, she would immediately think, "Oh my god. What did I do? Did I do something wrong?"

But deeply understanding that she wasn't in alignment with this person helped her to recalibrate her mindset and energy. It reduced the time she spent in self-doubt.

Now, Hilary is in a new role but still applying the Power Partners Formula™. She recently told me, "Work is just truly rewarding now because every conversation is fun, and the stress of wondering 'Will this person give? Do they like our work?' is nowhere near what it used to be. I don't necessarily raise money in every conversation, but it's a great feeling to have a wonderful conversation and then see the next donation increase."

Reflecting on her experiences, Hilary said, "It truly has been so rewarding. Learning how to lead with alignment changed everything."

Alignment Fundraising in Practice

Now that we understand how our beliefs and energy levels affect our connection with self and inner alignment, let's take it a step further to see how higher levels of anabolic energy directly affect our fundraising.

The two hypothetical fundraisers in this section have found themselves in a competition on a giving day. The first to persuade 10 existing donors to increase their annual gift wins an additional $10,000.

Our first fundraiser, Sandy, is enthusiastic and dedicated, yet scattered and feeling desperate. She can't stop worrying about the competition. Sandy works tirelessly, pursuing multiple avenues at once. She rummages through her customer relationship management system for past donation reports. She drafts a new call script and outgoing email template. She emails board members asking for referrals and personal outreach. She puts another meeting on the calendar to brainstorm new strategies with her team, even though they're already on a tight deadline. Despite her hard work, Sandy is always chasing her tail. She has several irons in the fire, but none of them is heating up. Three of her existing donors agree to increase their gifts, three decline, and the rest don't respond. Overwhelmed by her multitude of undertakings, Sandy finds herself stressed out and feeling defeated, with nothing but a chaotic, disorganized strategy to show for it.

Our second contestant is Marisol. Instead of focusing on the competition and diving headfirst into uncoordinated activities, Marisol starts by formulating a strategy. She identifies a group of 20 donors with whom she has great relationships and who are committed to the cause and are aligned with a particular element of her program. Given the way these donors have engaged before, she believes they would be excited by the opportunity to have their donation leveraged for an extra $10,000 for the organization. Marisol records a personal, heartfelt video of herself explaining her idea and the competition. Her video isn't polished or perfect, but it is authentic, passionate, and enthusiastic. Marisol sends the video to her selected donors, and within no time, she has all 10 pledges she needs to win the competition.

Sandy stresses; Marisol connects.

Sandy's actions are driven by pressure and fear, leading her to scatter her energy and resources over too many initiatives. The thought of *not* getting that $10,000 activates Sandy's reactive approach, making her throw everything at the wall instead of committing to one strategy.

This results in her frantic (and ultimately unsuccessful) pursuit of every potential opportunity.

When it's spelled out like this, it may be difficult to see why Sandy's panicked disorganized approach is the default for many fundraisers trying their hardest to create success. The reality is that Sandy's technique often feels safer. It gives an illusion of control and progress because we're visibly busy and ticking off tasks. The boost we get from feeling like we're making progress distracts from the reality of the situation: this is a reactive response, not a strategic response. This approach represents the current fundraising landscape, which often prompts catabolic energy and an overactivation of the nervous system that causes the body's fight, flight, or freeze response discussed in Chapter 3. Sandy was trying to press forward despite her catabolic energy, instead of realigning her mind and body into an anabolic state.

Marisol's anabolic energy enabled her to consider her organization's needs alongside the interests of her donors. She knew the way to create sustainable, reliable partnerships was through authentic relationships, so she began by identifying donors that have illustrated connection and commitment to real partnership in the past. Then she focused on nurturing those relationships in an aligned way that would create a clear win–win.

True success and alignment occur only when both sides are willing to understand and empathize with each other. Harnessing our energy and working from an anabolic state gives us the chance to operate with more clarity and confidence, naturally changing our focus toward alignment with our ideal partners. As mentioned previously, the hardest part of fundraising has always been threading the needle between raising money and building relationships. A lot of fundraising theories are constantly trying to find the balance between the two. But what if raising money always happens *through* aligned relationships? I think once we are able to truly focus on relationship-oriented fundraising strategies that focus on alignment, we begin to raise more money because it feels good for all involved. That's how we move more money with more ease.

Understanding Your Funders

To create an Alignment Fundraising strategy and identify potential Power Partners for our organizations, we need to understand our potential funders. We need to learn what motivates and inspires them and recognize any constraints they may be facing. Knowing their priorities enables us to map out the alignment between our organization and the people who support it.

Funders should not be lumped into one group and funneled through the same marketing or communication plan. Funders have different interests and motivations, and it is part of our job to translate our work into the perspectives of different constituent groups. Too many fundraisers treat all funders homogeneously, but they're not all the same. To help us avoid this mistake, we can consider the *funder lenses*. Funders and organizations, like all people, each have unique ways of viewing the world. By visualizing different types of funders wearing different colored lenses, we're reminded that funders' perceptions of reality, interests, and motivations affect how they view their impact and what they value in a nonprofit organization. The lenses influence their key priorities and where they can see alignment with our organization. For example, let's say foundations wear blue lenses and corporate partners wear red lenses. If we're describing something we see in red and using all red-toned language, the person who is wearing blue glasses won't be able to understand our version of reality, and therefore is not going to be able to connect with us.

To better recognize our funders' motivations, we can activate our empathy. *Empathy* is the action of understanding and becoming sensitive to another's feelings or experiences. It differs from sympathy—which is a surface-level grasp of someone's situation from our own perspective—in proximity to the subject. Sympathy places separation between the subject and the observer (Think: *I'm here and you're there*), whereas empathy closes the gap between the subject and the observer (Think: *We're in this together*).

For example, individuals who wish to contribute to a nonprofit that provides meals and supplies for cancer patients are motivated by their desire to help make the patient's journey more comfortable and less stressful. Fundraisers can empathize with the individual donors and build deeper relationships with them by engaging them throughout the process. Fundraisers can share photos, thank-you notes from patients, or other ways their contributions make the patient's experience more manageable.

Empathy is a powerful tool to cultivate strong, sustainable relationships with a diverse range of funders.

There are three broad categories of funders for us to consider, each with their own lenses: individual supporters, corporate contributors, and foundation funders (there is also a fourth funder type, government entities, but for the purpose of this discussion, we're focusing on the other three). Although there can be a lot of variation and overlap among them, it is helpful to illuminate in broad strokes the different motivations, incentives, and objectives that shape the lenses of each category of funders. This is key for assessing alignment.

Individual Supporters Individual donors often have personal motivations for giving, such as their personal beliefs and values, a deep connection to the cause, a relationship with someone involved in the organization, or a personal experience related to the nonprofit's mission. Individuals are looking for connection and a sense of belonging with others who share their passion for a particular cause. We are in a time of extreme disconnect as a society, but nonprofits can be a respite where groups of individuals can feel like they belong to something bigger and reconnect with a community of like-minded people.

Over the past decade, researchers have learned more about how disconnected and lonely people are. Creating strategies that give individuals the opportunity to form quality social connections can improve health and well-being. Acts of giving specifically can provide significant benefits and improve mental and physical health as connections deepen (Cohen 2023).

When I spoke to Woodrow Rosenbaum, Chief Data Officer for GivingTuesday, he pointed out two important factors in individual giving: large-scale donors started pulling back in 2022, which had a significant impact on the sector as a whole, and individuals are not being engaged equally by nonprofits (Rosenbaum 2024). There is a kind of vicious cycle of asking "fewer, more important people" to give, which "has diminishing returns, adds urgency, and pushes organizations to focus on large-donor stewardship at the expense of other engagement," Rosenbaum explained. Engagement campaigns like grassroots organizing take the hit when organizations shift their focus to the few wealthy potential contributors.

"The people who are not giving to nonprofits are probably pretty inclined to do so if they're made to feel like they matter," he said (Rosenbaum 2024). I agree, and believe that our challenge to engage potential donors signifies either a complete lack of communication or, when communication occurs, we're over-asking without any real connection or relationship building.

"Not being transactional and helping people feel like they're part of the mission is the recipe for getting good results," Rosenbaum said (Rosenbaum 2024). Strategies that have proven effective include "being in dialogue with your donors; not talking less, but talking more—just not using the same solicitations." These conversations can give people "lots of different on-ramps to the idea that you're building collectively." Building community means moving beyond self-interest, which is why inspiring generosity should be at the heart of individual donor engagement and connection.

When connecting with individual donors, they want to understand:

- Why your organization is different
- Why their particular involvement matters
- What their donation will help support
- How the organization affects the community or cause
- How to easily engage

These can all serve as talking points in initial engagement and follow-up conversations—both on an individual level and through segmented group communication. When building relationships with individuals, we need to demonstrate that we're in this together, and continue engaging them to show them how they can become part of the community beyond their initial connection. To do this, individual donors typically appreciate emotional storytelling, clear evidence of impact, and a personalized or personal touch.

The challenge, Rosenbaum pointed out, is not to convince people to be generous because generally, they are (Rosenbaum 2022). The challenge is to get them interested in the mission so they have the opportunity to show their generosity. Continuing to copy and paste messages of urgency, emergency, and financial crises will persuade some to give, but it's not a sustainable fundraising strategy. Plus, as we talked about previously, transactional fundraising methods are a recipe for fundraiser discomfort and chronic stress. Instead, for the individual, it comes back to genuine belonging, connections, and relationship-building. The good news is that this is better for fundraisers too.

As Seth Godin, best-selling author, entrepreneur, speaker, and teacher, said in our conversation about Power Partner principles,

> The most important thing to remember if you're a fundraiser, is that no one donates $100 to your cause unless it's worth $200 to them to do that. People aren't doing you a favor. They are buying something on sale: the feeling, the emotion, the connection, the magic for less than it costs.
>
> So, you're giving them an opportunity; you are not taking. With that said, "people like us do things like this" is the definition of culture. Not everybody is going to give money to any nonprofit. Doesn't matter which one it is. Everyone will not do it. Everyone will not drink a Coke. Everyone will not be a vegan. Everyone will not drive an electric car. Everyone is irrelevant. We are looking for someone.
>
> And one of the main reasons that someone does something is because they see identity and affiliation in doing it. (Godin 2022)

Corporate Contributors   Years ago, I found myself in an exciting cross-sector partnership with a marketing VP from a prominent Fortune 500 company. Over several weeks, we explored various ways our organizations might collaborate. Through our meetings, we formed a comfortable and friendly rapport, frequently discussing our shared enthusiasm for the work my nonprofit was engaged in.

In one of these meetings, there was a moment when the VP's demeanor shifted. He paused, his gaze dropping to his desk, and said, "I'm sorry to ask this, but could you tell me the number of subscribers on your email newsletter list? I apologize, but it's a detail my boss needs to know to justify the investment in this collaboration." I completely understood why he asked and I shared the number. I recognized that even though he genuinely believed in and wanted to support our mission, he also needed to justify the investment based on marketing metrics. These are the types of details that shape most corporate funder lenses.

Understanding this piece is important if you want to move beyond asking a company to sponsor a table at your event to building a more strategic partnership. To move in this direction, you need to ensure that working with companies is actually in alignment with the beliefs and values of your organization. It is not lost on me that many of the problems nonprofits are trying to address are created by companies that other nonprofits are trying to partner with. This is why for some nonprofits, corporate partnerships (or certain corporate partnerships) do not make sense because they are fundamentally misaligned with the goal of the organization. Before we can understand the lens of a corporate partner, we need to come to terms with whether or not they are right for our organization.

The difference between building a Power Partnership with a company and just asking for a monetary donation is rooted in a belief in mutual benefit (think of the win–win in Energy Level 5). It's through this orientation that we can see how corporations often engage in philanthropy for both altruistic and business reasons. Nonprofits align incentives with corporations by demonstrating how a partnership can meet the philanthropic goals of the corporation and provide visibility, branding, or other benefits that support their business interests.

Money donated by companies comes through three primary channels:

- The company's marketing budget
- Corporate social responsibility (CSR)
- A corporate foundation

Corporate partnerships—through marketing departments—often hold a lot of unexplored (and often unrestricted) resources for nonprofits where their investment is tied to marketing benefits, and the nonprofit can direct the funds however they need to inside their organization.

When engaging a corporation, keep in mind some of the goals their marketing team may have, and how you can provide this through your partnership. For example:

- Improving brand awareness and reputation
- Attracting top talent
- Increasing marketing/sales
- Aligning with business goals

When I spoke to Floyd Jones, social entrepreneur, creator, and founder of BackBlack, he talked about his passionate approach to building relationships with corporations:

I have worked with so many different corporate brands. Why? Because I understand there are so many people out there. You have to understand that the world is big, and if you're only looking at it through small lenses, that is all you're going to get. Abundance is real. We talk about abundance mindset all the time, but abundance mindset starts with asking. Just open up your mouth and ask the company down the street that aligns with your [organization]. Don't just ask some random [company]. . . . People always want to do good. . . . People want to get involved. They want to support. They want to help. They just need an avenue to do that. (Jones 2024)

Some companies also have a CSR department or team within the human resources department, whose mission is to create volunteer programs and outreach opportunities for employees. The CSR team will partner with nonprofits to increase employee engagement, morale, and retention through volunteer opportunities and gift matching; provide a motivating purpose for their company and employees through local partnerships; and increase employee skill development, team building, and leadership opportunities (Kerszenbaum 2023). Unfortunately, CSR partnerships often come without a sufficient budget, so be careful before promising a bunch of volunteer opportunities that will stretch your capacity without additional resources. For nonprofits, it's important to recognize and understand the interests of these partners—enhancing team cohesion, and reinforcing company culture (among others)—while being honest about your organization's capacity for this type of partnership and keeping community needs centered in the volunteer opportunities you offer.

Another common type of partnership opportunity with a company is through a company's corporate foundation. These entities share many similarities with other types of foundations, but their core difference lies in their primary motivations. Because they are sometimes an extension of their parent company, corporate foundations can align their philanthropy with opportunities that directly support their business objectives or the company's broader social responsibility goals, which can overlap with their environmental, social, and governance funding or CSR initiatives.

I share all of this to help you see something: companies are looking for nonprofit partners because nonprofits bring a lot of value to their relationships with prospective and current customers and employees. So, if you do think corporate partners are the right fit for your organization, make sure you present your value through their lens. Additionally, because of the web of overlapping motivations between different funding arms, it's always helpful to get curious with representatives at the company to find out where a potential partnership likely has the most alignment.

Foundation Funders Unlike individuals, whose giving is linked to their personal identity and motivations, or companies, which are incentivized by business goals, foundations are focused on strategic initiatives or issue areas and are usually interested in results-based interventions with specific goals and criteria in mind. Nonprofits can align incentives with foundations by emphasizing the expected outcomes of the partnership and demonstrating how their programs meet these criteria and further the overarching mission of the foundation through strategic alignment.

The first level of alignment between a foundation and a nonprofit is either direct mission alignment or peripheral mission alignment. *Direct mission alignment* is present when the foundation's grant priorities overlap exactly with a nonprofit's mission. For example, if a foundation is seeking to invest in cancer patient education and your organization provides cancer patient education, you have direct mission alignment.

Peripheral mission alignment leaves more wiggle room for organizations because foundations sometimes have a broad vision for their contributions, aligning with organizations across diverse focus areas. With peripheral mission alignment, as long as the mission of the nonprofit affects the foundation's mission, a partnership could still make sense. For example, if your organization's cancer patient education program aims to improve health equity for the community, and the foundation wishes to invest in health equity programs in that community, then peripheral mission alignment exists.

However, in both cases, we need to take things a step further to understand if there is tactical and strategic alignment in how the program is delivered, particularly through the lens of structure and approach to mission fulfillment. It needs to be said that ideally, foundations are using or moving toward trust-based philanthropy, where they respect that local communities and the organizations rooted in these communities know best how to achieve their goals. Foundations shouldn't dictate specific methods but should trust the expertise of those on the ground in their approach to mission fulfillment. However, that is not how it often works in the current foundation landscape, so I want to break down how many foundations view alignment for the fundraisers navigating this environment.

Here's an example of a situation where a foundation and a nonprofit have direct mission alignment but lack tactical and strategic alignment. Consider two approaches to combating loneliness among middle school students. One approach, used by a nonprofit, focuses on developing and distributing a virtual reality program that connects students with peers in a space free of judgment and social anxiety. Conversely, the foundation advocates for in-person gatherings, lunch meet-ups, and opportunities for face-to-face conversations based on its research on what combats loneliness most effectively.

Both the nonprofit and foundation share the desire to alleviate loneliness among students, which makes it seem like they would make good partners at first glance. However, their methods and interests show a divergence in strategy, using different tools to solve the same problem. In this case, the two would potentially not be effective Power Partners, despite the shared end goal. This isn't always the case, and it's worth a conversation, but in order to align, partners should ultimately share a mission and agree on the plan to achieve it. To truly identify alignment and ensure we're using our time effectively, we must take a closer look at how potential partners approach a problem rather than focusing solely on whether we are aligned with their intended mission outcome.

As we strive for alignment with foundations, I hope we work toward a philanthropic culture that values and trusts the expertise of local communities and nonprofits, allowing them to lead with their knowledge and experience.

The Illusion of "Easier" Fundraising

If you've been having trouble fundraising from specific types of funders, it might be because you're defaulting to opportunities that seem less intimidating, despite having only a loose alignment with your mission. Consider grants as a prime example: the allure of applying through open grant portals can impede the effectiveness of your overall fundraising strategy. When I began working closely with nonprofits, I found time and again that fundraisers were spending a lot of time submitting grant applications without first confirming strong alignment or the actual probability of receiving funds. Despite success rates as low as 2% to 3%, these organizations never questioned their approach. But when I would coach them about their fundraising strategy, the reason for submitting so many applications became clear. The welcoming nature of an open grant portal provided a false sense of security, making it feel less intimidating than reaching out to a cold contact or trying to build a deeper relationship with someone who might ultimately reject them. For many of us, a grant submission activates less fear because it offers the illusion of control and a perceived safe space to ask for money (after all, that's the point of a grant application).

Not all rejection feels the same, and for many of us, a grant not coming through when we didn't have a personal relationship feels less vulnerable than a human-to-human interaction. Applying for grants can feel safer because it protects some of the tender parts of ourselves and our organizations that feel so exposed during other forms of fundraising and relationship building. But an open grant portal is not an indicator of alignment—someone giving money and someone needing money are not the basis for a genuine funder relationship. This is important to remember with all types of funders because the tendency to choose seemingly less intimidating fundraising methods manifests in other scenarios as well, such as setting up informational booths at community events or casually presenting at local service clubs. These strategies appeal because they seem to minimize the risk of direct rejection or judgment, but they can also divert our time and energy away from pursuing more meaningful and aligned funding opportunities.

Each type of funder gives us the opportunity to create aligned partnerships in different ways. Understanding funder lenses provides nonprofit professionals with the ability to see our organizations from their different perspectives, and start to understand their wants and needs. By getting to know our funders, we start to truly identify how we can best partner with them and align them with our organization's assets that they will find most valuable.

But let's be clear: understanding and empathizing with our donors does not mean centering their needs over the community, organization, or ourselves. Don't abandon your mission, and don't abandon yourself. Mapping alignment and understanding your assets helps you stay true to yourself and your mission.

Mapping Alignment

In *What I Wish I Knew When I Was 20: A Crash Course on Making Your Place in the World*, Dr. Tina Seelig (2009b) recounted a story from her career teaching students at Stanford. After breaking into teams, Seelig gave each team a sealed envelope containing $5 of "seed funding." The goal was to transform the seed funding into as much money as possible. The teams could spend as much time planning as they wanted, but once they opened their envelopes, they only had two hours to implement their plans. At the end of the exercise, each team had three minutes to present their idea and share their results with the class.

Seelig saw brilliant ideas to turn the seed money into hundreds of dollars. One team booked reservations at busy restaurants and sold their spots to patrons who wanted to avoid a long wait. Another team offered to measure bicycle tire pressure for passing students and would refill them for $1. But the team that truly shocked Seelig thought about their assets in a completely different way. Rather than focus on how to spend their seed money, this team considered all the other assets they were given in Seelig's class. They decided to sell their three-minute presentation time to an outside company that was interested in recruiting Stanford students. The student team helped that company create a commercial, which aired during the time the students would have presented. The outside company got in front of their target audience, and the team made $650. According to Seelig, this team was successful because "they recognized that they had a fabulously valuable asset that others didn't even notice, just waiting to be mined" (Seelig 2009a).

As fundraisers, we commonly fall into the trap of thinking transactionally about our assets, or the value of our offer. However, we're so deeply entrenched in the lie that only money holds value that we can't see another perspective: funders are looking for our nonmonetary assets to create mutually beneficial partnerships.

Recognizing that money is far from the only thing of value, Seelig changed the "seed funding" in future projects, giving students ten paper clips instead of money and telling them to generate as much value (not necessarily money) as possible. Over the years, she has given teams different kinds of starting material, including sticky notes, rubber bands, and even unmatched socks. Regardless of what they start with, Seelig has continued to see brilliant outcomes when her students think broadly about their assets (Seelig 2009a).

You and Your Organization Have So Much Value (Beyond What You Think)

To create partnerships that are more than transactional, we need to think beyond the value of money alone. Nonprofits bring additional value and assets to the table, and often it's these assets that solidify long-term partnerships. Asset mapping aims to reorient the way fundraisers think about our own organizational assets and the abundance to which we already have access, and to identify funders who value these assets.

I spoke to Maurizio Zollo, Scientific Director of the Leonardo Centre on Business for Society at Imperial College Business School and Professor of Strategy and Sustainability, about the future of cross-sector partnerships. He said every NGO needs to think of themselves as the "suppliers to a fundamental good [or] service, where the private sector is on the demand side." He explained that the social maladies nonprofits have been created to solve, and are experts in, are now "recognized by the private sector as something that they need to do something about." This means there is an opportunity for nonprofits to leverage their expertise as a partnership asset. "There's no question, the demand is there. . . . And shifting the way we think about ourselves as the suppliers of solutions is a cultural shift, it puts the whole conversation on completely different grounds because it's a win-win for both, immediately" (Zollo 2021).

In 2023, I coached a group of Patagonia grantees about the concept of asset mapping. As they started to talk with each other about their organizations' assets, I could feel the energy in the room rise. This is the power of asset mapping: it not only helps us see where alignment does and does not exist, but it shifts the energy and power dynamics in the relationship as we move out of scarcity mindset. Trying to "think abundantly" can be overwhelming for fundraisers because it feels so far away from our daily experience. Asset mapping enables us to transition from scarcity toward abundance because we start to see and understand all of the value we bring to the table and the resources already available inside our organizations.

Your Inventory of Assets

Asset-based strategies play an important role in the sector, with many experts advocating for a more positive, strengths-based approach to programming, marketing, partnership building, and fundraising.

Your organizational assets can be internal or external, and different types of assets are valuable to different types of funders. Each asset is one component in the organization's unique alchemy, which can be like a magnet that attracts funding from the right donors.

Here are some examples of assets your organization might have:

- Social media following or the number of people on your email list
- Cause marketing opportunities
- Volunteer opportunities
- A story about a beneficiary directly affected
- One-to-one direct giving opportunities
- Strong impact data and metrics
- Thought leaders on your board of directors

Asset mapping is fundraiser-friendly because it's not about cutting further into your limited time to create new assets that check every box for every type of funder. Instead, it enables us to see and value what we already have and then asks us to focus on which assets each type of funder is looking for that are already available. From there, we can prioritize funders based on where asset alignment already exists and connect those assets to funders who need them.

Although this exchange might sound transactional or feel tit-for-tat, the shift from a transactional mindset to one centered on mutual benefits and deep connections means that it's not about a simple exchange of money for services or assets, but about forging partnerships in which both parties are invested in the impact of their collaboration. This type of partnership is rooted in the belief that our shared success in achieving our collective goals supports us all far beyond the transaction itself. Creating asset maps brings us one step closer to forming aligned partnerships.

Matching Funders and Assets

Once we have a clear picture of our funders' lenses and our organization's assets, we can see where we align and prioritize funders and outreach based on how well they complement the organization.

Let's take the assets I listed previously and give an example of how you could map them to potential funders (see Table 5.1).

Table 5.1   Asset Mapping Example

Asset	Which Type of Funder Is the *Most* Interested in This Asset?
Social media following or the number of people on your email list	Corporate (marketing)
Cause marketing opportunities	Corporate (brand/marketing)
Volunteer opportunities	Individuals and corporate (CSR)
Story about a single beneficiary directly impacted	Individual
One-to-one direct giving opportunities	Individual
Strong impact data and metrics	Foundation
Thought leaders on your board of directors	Foundation

Here's an example of how you would align an email list asset with a potential corporate partner: Because corporations want to engage with as many new potential customers as possible, sending emails to your list that feature your partner's message, logo, featured product, or promotion is enticing to their marketing teams. Collaborations like this provide a win for your organization, your partner, and your audience, as long as the offer or company's message aligns with your audience. Your partner gets to showcase their brand in front of your audience, your audience discovers offerings that resonate with their interests, and your organization gains support. It's a synergy where everyone benefits—your nonprofit, your corporate partner, and, most important, your community.

Here's another example of how thought leaders on your board of directors could align with foundations: if you have a board of directors filled with prominent community members that have their finger on the pulse in an aligned issue area, their insights could be extremely valuable to a foundation. Opportunities that would bring together the foundation and those board members—like hosting a networking or educational event—could be invaluable to your foundation partner and something they would be excited to fund. The foundation would gain access to top-tier expertise that would enhance the impact of their initiatives, and your organization, in turn, would receive support and recognition, elevating your reach.

Duke Stump, marketing expert and founder of Bonfire with Soul, said it best, "I think the beauty of partnerships and collaborations is that they're rich because ... you're also bringing a diversity of different thoughts in, which I always think helps. You can get out of your own monoculture of thinking. So much is about partnerships and this mutualistic approach, in a way that ... both parties benefit without detracting from the other" (Stump 2021).

Case Study: Heather Hooper

Her Fundraising Transformation

Heather Hooper is an executive director for the Dementia Alliance of North Carolina, where she and her team provide resources and assistance for patients and families affected by the disease. There are many opportunities for partnerships with funders in the corporate sector interested in helping to address an issue affecting 55 million people worldwide.

Heather joined the Power Partners Formula™ program because she saw the untapped potential for corporate partnerships and wanted to develop a better outreach strategy. Heather had tunnel vision: she focused on events, exchanges, and engraved donor plaques. As so many fundraisers do, Heather saw money as something funders had that she did not. Although she knew many funders wanted to make a difference for people struggling with dementia, she assumed she could only offer them a seat at a fancy party in return. Typically, this meant that Heather would offer a potential donor the ability to sponsor a gala or to be featured in a series of social media posts.

This strategy worked to an extent. Before we started working together, Heather had secured a brand-new partnership that committed to giving $15,000 annually. After creating an asset map together, we discovered one of the organization's main assets was access to patients and caregivers. Doctors, pharmaceutical companies, and volunteers wanted visibility and networking opportunities with this audience.

So, Heather started tailoring and highlighting this asset in all of her communications to corporate donors. With the asset clearly articulated and the value to the donor clearly illustrated, Heather felt confident enough to put a proposal in front of that same $15,000 funder for $140,000.

They loved her offer and over the next year, grew their investment first to $95,000, then again to $200,000.

"Being able to clarify what those assets are has allowed us to package our offerings differently and go beyond offering just to be a walk sponsor," Heather said. "Now, we're doing these health care outreach initiatives. We've identified that one of our benefits for our health care provider outreach is putting collateral in a folder we're giving to physicians. Our donors love this and are willing to put dollars toward it."

I received a text from Heather about a different funder, and was so happy to celebrate with her on all fronts. Her confidence and approach to aligned funders shines through. She wrote, "Mallory! I just found out I got a $48,000 grant! It was with a foundation that aligned with our org so well. The lead reviewer also said it was one of the best proposals he has ever reviewed! Thanks for all your help and encouragement to help us get clear on what and who to ask!"

During a conversation about influence, Dr. Vanessa Bohns shared insights that help explain Heather's experience. As a social psychologist, professor of organizational behavior at Cornell University, and author of *You Have More Influence Than You Think: How We Underestimate Our Power of Persuasion, and Why It Matters* (2021), she identified a common oversight. When we go out and ask people for help, we often forget the value of our ask. But, as Bohns says, when fundraisers can overcome their fear of the vulnerability it takes to ask someone for something and step into a place of offering connection, we can "connect to where our potential funders are at, what they care about, the way they view the world, and the change they're trying to make." This is important because "people ultimately don't want to say no to you—they want to connect" (Bohns 2022).

By prioritizing funders based on how well they align with our organization's mission, values, and assets, we ensure our partnership offering will highlight what the funder cares about most from the beginning. From the first outreach, we're showing the potential partner we care about building mutually beneficial relationships.

Not All Money Is Created Equal

It is easy to get distracted by dollar signs, but as we've seen, accepting money from misaligned partners does not bring long-term stability to an organization. Before securing any partnership, we need to be clear on our funding needs and identify the most aligned partners for each initiative.

Once an organization clarifies its mission, values, and funding objectives, it can create norms, policies, and guidelines (like a gift acceptance policy) for identifying potential partners. This allows fundraisers to proactively prioritize appropriate partnerships while avoiding misaligned ones.

Yes, our organizations need to raise money, but saying no to the wrong partners will protect our energy and create space for the right yeses. When we clarify who our aligned partners are, our fundraising becomes easier to implement because we operate from a place of confidence instead of overwhelm and scarcity. Focusing on alignment decreases our fundraising fears and stress, enabling effective action from a more anabolic state.

Plus, when we shift into anabolic energy, we can more easily identify alignment, which in turn helps us experience anabolic energy more often. With this awareness, we can create cognitive loops that work in our favor instead of against us.

Creating an aligned fundraising strategy involves putting the right pieces together. Taking time to evaluate our approach and partner choices leads to easier prospecting, aligned partnerships, clear strategies, and long-term success. Once we identify the right partners for our organization, we can focus on building connected relationships with them.

6 | Building Connected Relationships

I've come a long way from the community garden, when my boss directed me to "just build relationships" and sent me on my way. It's true that relationships are key to fundraising; we know that strong relationships give us the opportunity to grow and expand our fundraising potential, our networks, and visibility for our organizations. But we want strong, *connected* relationships. *Connected relationships* happen when aligned funders and fundraisers develop a symbiotic relationship that grows and expands over time. Focusing our time and energy on building these relationships helps ease the stress of uncertainty and creates more opportunities for a funder to connect with the cause beyond a one-time monetary donation. Creating connected relationships starts with building trust from day one, following up with effective engagement touchpoints, and offering opportunities for dialogue.

Trust is an essential prerequisite for forging deep and meaningful connections. Research shows that without trust, we will face constant barriers to forming strong relationships (Wilkins 2018). But what does trust really look like? And how do we build it? Trust is "such a simple and complex word all at once," seemingly easy to achieve but often elusive and difficult to repair once it's been broken (RKD Group n.d.).

Trust is present in connections where both parties are comfortable being their authentic selves, confident in each other's decision-making and follow-through, and have empathy for one another. Researchers, including Frances Frei and Anne Morriss of the *Harvard Business Review* (2020) and members of Trusted Advisor Associates (2020), have identified several factors that drive trust:

- **Authenticity.** You share yourself. I know you're showing me the real you.
- **Logic.** You make the right decisions. I believe in your ability to think through and make reasoned judgments.
- **Empathy.** You care about me. I am confident you want me to succeed.
- **Credibility.** Your words are believable. When you say something, I know I can depend on the information.
- **Reliability.** Your actions are consistent. I can count on you to see something through.
- **Intimacy.** You feel safe. I feel comfortable confiding sensitive information with you.
- **Self-orientation.** You pay attention to me. I know you'll give me the time I need.

We've already discussed or alluded to several of these characteristics throughout the book, particularly authenticity, empathy, and reliability. But all of these characteristics are the foundational elements that replace transactional fundraising practices. When we as fundraisers can bring these elements into different communication channels and funder meetings, we connect with our Power Partners more easily.

Trust in Nonprofits

When it comes to nonprofits, trust can refer to feelings of confidence in another person to make the right decisions, a belief in the efficacy of another person, or feelings of faith in the organization as a whole

(Galford and Drapeau 2003). For our purposes, we can focus on two forms of trust between the fundraiser and the funder: organizational trust and personal trust. *Organizational trust* extends beyond the individual fundraiser and encompasses the donor's trust in the nonprofit organization, the nonprofit sector as a whole, and society itself. In a nationwide survey exploring the factors that create and break trust in civil society, Independent Sector, a coalition of changemakers, nonprofits, foundations, and corporations in the United States (2021), found that 83% of respondents said a nonprofit must earn their trust before they would be willing to support it.

"Public trust is the currency of the nonprofit sector" (Independent Sector 2021, 4). Those in the nonprofit sector are fueled by a commitment to making the world a better place, to turn generosity into life-changing services and outcomes that advance humanity. When the public gives to the nonprofit sector, it is with a belief in our ability and integrity to uphold these values and make the impact we have promised. Because misinformation and disinformation are significant drivers of declines in trust (Edelman Trust Barometer 2023), we must double down on our efforts to engage in clear, transparent, and consistent communication, starting with reliable and credible messages (Galford and Drapeau 2003). Without trust, the relationship between donors and organizations is fundamentally broken.

Now, is the scrutiny placed on nonprofits often unfair? Yes. Is there a problematic paternalistic tone and attitude in discussions of nonprofits being trustworthy or untrustworthy? Double yes. Nonetheless, operating in alignment requires strong, authentic connections between fundraisers and funders, and that does necessitate trust—just like in any healthy relationship.

To build trust that prioritizes human connection rather than viewing it as a checkbox that verifies our legitimacy, we can focus on personal trust. Have you ever met someone and felt, instinctively, that you could trust them? This form of trust, *personal trust*, is the trust we have in an individual. You might call it intuition or a gut feeling. Research indicates that trust is a fundamental human trait, influenced by our inherent need to form connections and build communities (Chavis and Lee 2015). This is because "working together has always been key to the survival of our species. Having faith in one another is in the best interest of the individual and the collective—especially in times of risk and uncertainty" (Bergland 2015). Imaging has revealed activations in the parts of the brain that deal with reward processing and positive emotions when you feel trust toward another person. Trusting each other literally makes us feel good.

Dr. Paul J. Zak, a neuroscientist and author of *Trust Factor: The Science of Creating High-Performance Companies* (2017b) conducted research that demonstrates how our brains produce oxytocin, a hormone associated with positive feelings, when we encounter someone whom we find trustworthy (Zak 2017a). Zak researched the relationship between oxytocin and trust for a decade, identifying measurable behaviors that produce trust in the workplace, such as recognizing excellence, allowing autonomy in how people perform their job functions, and encouraging employees to grow professionally and personally.

Two of Zak's findings are especially relevant for fundraising: (1) you can generate trust when you show vulnerability and intentionally build relationships with others, and (2) trust is the cornerstone of relationship building (Zak 2017a). We know identifying alignment is key, but we need to further explore the ingredients for deepening alignment by building connected relationships.

Building Real Relationships

To understand how we intentionally build real relationships between funders and fundraisers, I connected with Dr. Carole Robin. She is the cofounder of Leaders in Tech and coauthor of *Connect: Building Exceptional Relationships with Family, Friends, and Colleagues* (Bradford and Robin 2021). This work is based on Stanford Business School's *Interpersonal Dynamics* course. Bradford and Robin's years of research suggest relationships exist on a continuum. Each of the following six pillars demonstrates how we need to show up to create connected and rewarding relationships:

- You can be more fully yourself, and so can the other person.
- Both of you are willing to be vulnerable.
- You trust that self-disclosures will not be used against you.
- You can be honest with each other.
- You deal with conflict productively.
- Both of you are committed to each other's growth and development (Bradford and Robin 2021).

When I think about my most aligned funder relationships over the years, all six pillars have been present. Using the pillars as a framework, we can create lasting bonds with funders. Nonprofit work is a journey, and we want funders to feel invested in coming along with us. Showcasing our personality and passion while giving funders the opportunity to share as well creates the foundation of a healthy relationship.

Authenticity and Vulnerability

In our conversation, Robin said, "I don't have to hide behind a spun image, and I don't have to pretend to be somebody I'm really not" (Robin 2023). Fundraisers often feel intense pressure to present a perfectly curated front to potential funders. As discussed in Chapter 3, instances of rejection and persistent uncertainty can wreak havoc on our emotions and nervous system. Perfectionism can feel like armor against an impending rejection; however, not only is perfection an illusion but it also actually ends up creating a barrier between us and our funder in a way that dysregulates us and erodes trust. It's impossible to form a truly authentic connection with another person without letting them see who you really are. We don't have to divulge our innermost worries and deepest secrets, but we do have to be truthful about what we know, think, and feel. And, critically, we have to drop the facade of perfectionism.

The more we demonstrate vulnerability, the more space it creates for the funder to be vulnerable too. When I am about to invite someone to invest in an organization, I lead with openness by asking for permission to talk about money. I will often say something like, "The next part of the conversation always makes me the most nervous because I don't want to do anything that makes you think I'm not grateful for everything you've already done for our organization. But I also know this is the most sacred part of my job and important for our shared goal of _____. Are you open to talking about your level of investment in the organization this year?" My candidness about my discomfort creates space for the funder to be vulnerable too and to know I am entering the conversation with care.

As Robin pointed out, "If I play my cards really close, you're going to play yours even closer. And we'll never get to know anything about each other" (Robin 2023).

Honesty and Dealing with Conflict Productively

Connected relationships aren't immune to conflict. On the contrary, a pillar of strong connections is being willing to give honest feedback. Robin offered an example, "When you've done something that has hurt my feelings, or I think is really hurting our team or our cause, I don't worry that saying that to you will harm our relationship. In fact, I believe it will make our relationship even stronger" (Robin 2023).

We often fear hard conversations with our donors, worrying that politely pushing back against a suggestion may harm the relationship. In Chapter 2, I mentioned that I often hear fundraisers tell me they have "good" relationships with their funders, but when I begin to ask questions about why they are pursuing a program that isn't in alignment with their mission, they confess it was something the funder wanted, and they didn't want to create tension by suggesting an alternative approach.

This is a reflection of the scarcity mindset that leads to transactional fundraising and toxic power dynamics. Ultimately, this pulls you away from potential alignment with the funder. I brought up this example when talking with Dr. Vanessa Bohns, and she suggested people in positions of power often *hope* we will bring up questions that could create more efficient and equitable outcomes. "We worry that if we challenge [them], the whole thing is going to blow up and it's going to end in us having nothing. But that's not usually the way that it goes. Usually, you can ask for things in ways that really further the conversation" (Bohns 2022).

Being afraid of hard conversations is understandable, but it's not the way to foster a genuine connection or stay in alignment. When we're honest and share our knowledge and insights with the goal of advancing alignment, we build deeper relationships that lead to more impactful outcomes.

Case Study: Stacey Levy

The Power of Authentic Connections

Stacey Levy is an accidental fundraiser. She's dedicated her life to the organization she founded, Ellie's Army, in honor of her daughter. Ellie Levy was born with cystic fibrosis, a terminal genetic illness that mostly affects the lungs. Even in the face of profound obstacles, including two double lung transplants, Ellie stayed optimistic, kept her sense of humor, and continued her service for others. Before Ellie passed away in 2014 from complications of her illness, she helped start an effort to ensure others with cystic fibrosis could receive high-quality medical care. Several years later, Stacey expanded the organization's work and renamed the nonprofit to help children and young adults with all life-threatening illnesses—not just cystic fibrosis—in Ellie's honor.

Since 2017, Ellie's Army has given more than $780,000 in grants, helping more than 191 families and 7,000 individuals affected by life-threatening illnesses.

(continued)

(*continued*)

Although Stacey was steadfast in her commitment to Ellie's Army and fueled by an unstoppable motivation to support the work, she often struggled with her role as a fundraiser. "I felt like I was always asking for money, and I wasn't a good asker. I always felt uncomfortable," she said. She stopped feeling this way when she stopped seeing the donor as someone with the money that she needed and started to focus instead on the relationship and opportunities they could build together. "The idea of being authentic and valuing relationships was one thing that really transformed my fundraising."

Stacey learned how to tap into her anabolic energy and prioritize alignment when crafting emails to prospective funders. She allowed herself to be known by funders by being her true self, "sharing personally what the work means to me."

Stacey realized she had a unique ability to connect with others who might have experiences with illnesses like cystic fibrosis but learned she could only form those bonds when she shared her own experiences. This made space for the donors to feel like they could be vulnerable as well, unlocking opportunities to explore new paths forward. Stacey also learned how to share these stories with data that highlights the impact of her organization's work, which both underscored the work of the organization and helped to enhance trust by showing transparency and reliability.

In many ways, Stacey's story is like mine. Before using Alignment Fundraising, she was overwhelmed by asking people for money, and yet needed money to make the impact she desired. She now understands that this positive, confident anabolic energy lets her build better, stronger, and more financially viable relationships. And those relationships ultimately help her accomplish Ellie's Army's mission: to create a world in which every child and young adult has access to the best chance of survival, regardless of financial costs.

Connection in Practice

Usually, when we talk about *donor engagement*, we refer to metrics that show us how donors interact with our organization. We track their participation, communication style, follow-ups, retention, motivations, and assets. Unfortunately, we often think of engagement as a one-way conversation—asking questions like "Did they open my email?" "Did they click the link?" "Are they demonstrating that they care about what I am saying?"—instead of measuring the dialogue we're having. I understand that we have limited capacity to engage one-on-one with all our donors, but that doesn't mean there aren't opportunities for community dialogue, feedback, or personalized touchpoints with everyone. We need to think beyond engagement and recognize that what we really want is to create connection. Otherwise, our donor engagement strategies are transactional. Effective engagement and connection not only require us to think about what we're saying but also necessitate that we're allowing space for the donor to be seen and heard, as we would in any real relationship.

As Floyd Jones reminded me, "Alignment determines your assignment. How do you go deeper with the people that you already have? We can't just talk about transformation, but not have a path for them to transform. . . . Take your people deeper" (Jones 2024).

But the question is, how?

Jones gives us a few examples. "Maybe they go to an event. Well, how do you say, 'OK, you went to that event. Can you help me plan this next event now?' . . . Or, 'Hey, you work at this company, and I noticed that your company does corporate giving.'" But Jones didn't stop there when he was trying to take his donors deeper. "I researched every single volunteer that I had, and I asked them what company [they] worked at. And then I did a major search on what companies do CSR practices that are aligned with what we're doing and I wrote the letters [to the CSR lead from the volunteer] for them" (Jones 2024).

As Jones makes clear, if we want our donors to be excited about the invitation to join our work in deeper ways, we have to show that we're also eager to explore the promise of the partnership. Similar to the processes we used to identify alignment (funder lenses and asset mapping), we can develop our communication and connection approach based on the potential donor type using what we know about their interests and motivations.

Effective Engagement

The moment someone steps into our sphere or transitions into a donor, we want to be in conversation, further developing the relationship. This involves an ongoing web of communication often referred to as the *donor journey*, which focuses on a donor's involvement and relationship with an organization. There is a lot of literature detailing how to create strong donor journeys, and I encourage you to combine those recommendations with the principles of connection, trust, and relationship building that we explore in this book. I'd also encourage you to be wary of thinking about donor journeys as a "stream" of communication. When we do that we're back to things flowing in one direction instead of facilitating actual connection and dialogue. Although we all love the linear and predictable nature of a stream, effective engagement and real connection happens in a web, interconnecting communications with other methods of outreach and feedback, participation, referrals, and contributions from donors.

For individual donors, whether we are reaching out to someone one-on-one or we're designing mass communications to a group of people, we want to start by answering foundational questions to ensure that we're prioritizing alignment in our outreach. For individuals in particular, you want to think about these questions:

- Whom are we trying to engage and be in conversation with?
- What do we know about them?
- What do we want them to know?
- What are the best ways (message and modality) to be in dialogue with them?
- What types of opportunities might they be most interested in to go deeper with the organization?

When it comes to corporate partnerships, however, once we determine alignment with a company, we want to be able to clearly show corporate partners what a partnership with us will look like, and how it will benefit them and meet their priorities. In all of your messaging efforts, you want to highlight the opportunities your organization brings. Gather examples of how you align with their incentives and be clear about what assets you have that you believe will be the most interesting to them. As mentioned previously, lead with your value and where you specifically see alignment to demonstrate that you are interested in a mutually beneficial partnership.

Building connections and relationships with foundations can seem a little more streamlined and structured than with individuals and corporate partners, but it's important to not lose sight of the relationship. Generally, foundations will follow either an open application or closed application process. In an *open application* process, any eligible organization can submit a funding application. However, prior to submitting an application, I highly encourage you to try to schedule a meeting with someone from the foundation. At the end of the day, all funding comes from relationships, and if there is an opportunity to connect human to human, we want that opportunity. A *closed application* process, by contrast, is by invitation only. Foundations operating under this model have specific criteria and objectives, and they actively seek out organizations that align with their goals.

Truly connected relationships require us to listen to the other person and ensure they feel seen, so it's essential that fundraisers respect the requests on a foundation's website and do not submit applications when we're not invited or don't meet the criteria. That being said, a closed application process does not always mean that there isn't any opportunity to connect. Sometimes a foundation might be open to meeting with new organizations to learn more about our work and potentially invite us to submit an application in the future. When we find a foundation that we believe is strongly aligned (and it doesn't say not to contact them), we can reach out to a staff member explaining why we want to meet, and see if they would be open to an introductory call. It's always good to mention that we understand they don't take unsolicited proposals, but we'd like to see if our organization might fit into their funding priorities in the future.

Reaching Out to Aligned Prospects

When we're reaching out to prospects focused on alignment, we are not trying to get every single funder to meet with us or fund us; we are genuinely trying to figure out if alignment exists. In the email outreach we do inside Power Partners, there is always a line in the emails to the effect of "Given the alignment I saw with _____, I wanted to make sure to reach out, but it is no problem if you aren't interested in meeting or aren't open to exploring partnership." We include this in our outreach because we want to make it clear that we're not interested in their money at all costs and we don't want them to invest if it is not the right fit.

When I originally started to put those caveats in my emails, an interesting thing happened: more people started to say yes to an initial meeting. Why? Because they could tell that I was focused on alignment and not money. Alignment means giving people the option to say no, while making it clear we only want to move forward if it feels good to both sides. After using this approach for years, I found that research supports this: giving people the opportunity to say no actually makes it more likely they will say yes (Schlund et al. 2024). At the end of the day, it reinforces one of my core beliefs: when fundraising feels better to us, it feels better to the funder, too.

But remember, regardless of how great your outreach is, people are busy. That means effective engagement often requires a series of follow-up communications. Whether it's sending out multiple reminders for a community event via bulk email or revisiting your initial outreach to a potential corporate partner, considerate persistence is key. Beware of falling into the trap of thinking, "If they were truly interested, they would have acted on my first invitation." Keep in mind, a lack of response is not necessarily about their lack of interest; they might just be swamped. Always be ready to follow up and prompt again. Plan for this so the lack of a quick response doesn't turn into an internal narrative rooted in self-doubt. When we shift expectations like this, we get out in front of internal Energy Blocks and are able to maintain a higher average energy level throughout the year.

The Myth of Donor Fatigue

It's common to hear fundraisers say things like, "Our donors don't want to hear from us," "Our donors are unsubscribing, so we need to communicate less," or "Because we don't get responses from our donors, they must not want to be involved in our organization anymore."

This presumption is a fear of donor fatigue—a state where donors, bombarded with incessant requests, become desensitized and less willing to contribute. I have always had mixed feelings about the conversation on donor fatigue, so I asked Woodrow Rosenbaum about combatting this issue. He said, "The data does not support that donor fatigue is a thing. Donors are not tired of giving, but they might be tired of your message" (Rosenbaum 2022).

In our pursuit of immediate fundraising results, we disregard what's necessary to cultivate lasting relationships with our donors. This is why we are dealing with unpredictable donations and donor disengagement, and funders are feeling hounded for funds or disconnected from the organization's core mission. But let's be clear, it's not a weariness of connecting that's driving donors away. More often, it's the transactional nature of the interactions—the missing quality and relevance of the messages being conveyed—that dampens their enthusiasm.

Preparing for Funder Meetings

I often see fundraisers spend hours preparing what they'll say in a meeting with a donor, but they forget to reserve time to prepare themselves energetically for the meeting. Our energy, which is often conveyed through our body language and tone, affects how our words are received. How we deliver our ideas is just as important, if not more so, than the actual words we say. We want to enter meetings with our desired energy so our body language and tone match what we're trying to get across with our words. To help with this, use the tools in Chapter 4. As a reminder, those tools involve creating consciousness and curiosity about our limiting beliefs, interpretations, and assumptions. They also include additional techniques for raising our anabolic energy to access Energy Levels 5, 6, and 7, through methods such as acknowledging, validating, and distanced self-talk. We may use the same script or talking points at Energy Level 1 as Energy Level 5, but the person receiving the message will hear it differently based on our tone and approach to the conversation.

Another way to ensure you go into a meeting with your desired energy is to have your goals match the articulated goals of the meeting. Sounds simple, but it's a step often missed. If you said that you wanted to get the funder's feedback on something, you need to ask for their feedback. If you told them you wanted to tell them about a new program, you need to be ready to do that. Did you say you weren't going to ask them for money? Don't! (Unless they ask and lead you there themselves.) Alignment is about staying true to our intention and word—our behavior needs to match our communication. The moment we have a different internal intention than the one we have communicated with the donor, we are out of alignment with ourselves and with them. This is another example of how alignment and trust are interconnected.

Making the Offer

Assuming we've invited the donor to a meeting where it's clear we're going to talk about investment in our organization, we find ourselves in a position to make a specific invitation. Because we've been focused on alignment from the start, we can plan for the meeting with confidence, knowing that the donor is interested and open to discussing potential avenues to invest in our work. Although the Power Partners mantra is that great fundraising isn't an ask, it's an offer, you'll notice that I use different terms interchangeably (ask/offer, donate/invest). Ultimately, the actions are all the same, so use the terms that feel most empowering to you. Regardless of the terminology, it's crucial to create an environment where funders can make conscious choices about their involvement.

In funding meetings, a lot of fundraisers fall into perfectionist and people-pleasing tendencies because we're so close to getting funding that our fear and scarcity mindset create a myopic focus. To avoid these traps while providing necessary information to the funder, we need to prepare for open and transparent conversations.

In the Power Partners Formula™, I walk my clients through a detailed ask strategy for each type of funder that's a bit like a Choose Your Own Adventure with a bunch of if-then options. For our purposes, we'll review the main takeaways: Start each meeting by setting priorities, then discuss why you believe there is a potentially aligned partnership. From there, invite them to learn more about investment options or additional projects, then ask if they're open to hearing more about a particular investment level. At that point, you can make a specific invitation for funding.

As an example, here are some additional details about how this conversation flow might break down for individual donors in particular.

You start by catching up, sharing recent accomplishments in the organization, and (if they've donated before) reminding them of the impact of their last gift. After discussing your organization's impact and alignment with what you know about the donor's interests, you can transition to the offer with a bridge statement like, "I have loved watching you get so excited about our work on x. It seems like you are really aligned with our goal of x. So, I'm wondering if you'd be open to hearing a bit more about what we're thinking for the year ahead, and what it might look like to get involved with us in this work."

At this stage, you are asking for permission to proceed with the conversation. This permission is critical for both the donor's buy-in and ensuring they are making a conscious choice and not feeling unduly pressured. This is how we stay connected even in these vulnerable and tender moments. If they say yes, you can share more about your goals and vision for the area of your work where they are most aligned—here you need to be specific and tangible, making it clear what impact an investment would make on the outcomes you both desire. Then you ask for permission again. "I love seeing our alignment with our shared vision and the strategic goals I just outlined. Is this an area you're open to investing in?"

If they say yes, it's time to be clear, specific, and direct. You do not want to create any ambiguity about what you're asking for. This could sound like, "In order to do what I just outlined, it's going to take $250,000 to enable us to [specific action], which will ensure that [specific benefit or outcome]. We're looking for five funders to join us at the $50,000 investment level. Would you consider becoming one of those key supporters that helps us [specific action]?"

After you invite the donor to participate, stop talking. Wait and hold space for the donor to process and respond. This silence might be one of the hardest elements of a meeting like this, but it is crucial—do not present a caveat or justification or talk over them.

If they have questions, answer their questions honestly and help them understand why you believe there are mutually beneficial outcomes through a partnership. If the amount is different than what the donor has the capacity for, provide options like "I hear you that you can't do $50,000 this year. Would a contribution of $x be something you're comfortable with, or would you like to discuss other levels of support or ways to contribute?" or "I understand you can't do $50,000 this year. There are several ways you can support this effort, including [Option A] at $x, [Option B] at $y, and [Option C] that involves [nonmonetary contribution]. What aligns best with your interests?"

Again, give them space to respond, but also recognize they might not be able to give you an answer right then and there. Before the meeting ends you can say something like "I understand it's a significant decision. Would it be helpful if I provide more details about what your support would enable or the specific outcomes we anticipate?"

Maybe you've answered a bunch of questions and they need to take it back to all of the decision-makers. In that case, you could say, "I understand this is an important decision, and I want you to feel confident and excited about your support. I am so grateful for all of your past support and that you are considering this. Would it be alright if I followed up with you [suggest a time frame]?" You can also offer to schedule a follow-up meeting at that moment, which provides a specific time frame for the donor's decision-making and leverages the enthusiasm they are feeling in the current meeting. This approach will also save both of you from the time-consuming process of coordinating a follow-up meeting via email later.

Don't forget to communicate gratitude, focus on alignment, and connect from your anabolic energy. If you're talking to a corporate partner or foundation, remember to frame this conversation in terms of the areas in which they align with your organization (don't forget the funder's lens) and you'll also want to leverage the assets that you have that they are the most interested in. Clear communication sets expectations on both sides to facilitate a long-lasting, healthy relationship.

The Funder Says Yes, Now What?

Let's say your new Power Partner said yes to your partnership invitation—they are going to invest in your organization. This is great news! However, there are some pitfalls we need to be aware of: Oftentimes, after we cross this threshold with a donor, we deprioritize our relationship with them. Although we might offer initial gratitude for the funder's investment, and ensure benefit fulfillment if it's a corporate sponsor, our relationship with them can inadvertently drop down our priority list now that we've secured their support because our motivation to keep that funder as closely engaged wanes. This behavior doesn't feel good to anyone involved and has a huge impact on donor retention and the long-term sustainability of our fundraising efforts.

Retention refers to keeping a first-time donor or an annual donor engaged with the organization. Unfortunately, individual donor retention has steadily decreased over the past several years (Fundraising

Effectiveness Project 2023). On average, nonprofits retain only 51% of major donors. The number is especially stark for small donors (who give between $101.00 and $500.00), where nonprofits retain only 38% from the previous year (Fundraising Effectiveness Project 2023). I think we need to be careful about how we track and talk about retention (because it can turn into another transactional way we think about fundraising), but I do believe it's important to reflect on what our donor retention number might tell us about our behavior. Our retention numbers encourage us to get curious about what we have or haven't done to lead to those results. Remember, donor behavior is a response. For many, donor retention numbers suggest a breakdown in modes of *stewardship*, the process by which a nonprofit continually engages a donor in order to keep them involved in the organization after a gift.

I often hear from fundraisers that they don't prioritize stewardship (and therefore retention) because they don't have enough time. However, I think one of the main reasons actually relates back to fear. Even though we have engaged the funder and received a donation, we often fall back into a scarcity mindset and transactional fundraising that leads to feelings of uncertainty about the strength of the relationship. Remember, our energy levels and motivation oscillate, so it is understandable that we fall back into feelings of self-doubt, especially when we aren't sure of the next steps with a donor or don't feel like we're on track with our overarching fundraising goal. When our self-doubt and inner chatter continue and overwhelm ensues, we stop engaging as often with the funder. These actions can contribute to the low retention numbers we see across the sector and the disconnection we feel with our donors.

My conversation with Dr. Szu-chi Huang, Associate Professor of Marketing at the Graduate School of Business at Stanford University, further explores the relationship between self-doubt, motivation, and connection and how that could be influencing our stewardship and retention trends.

In a sense, when I feel that I'm not doing that well—when I have that fear—that is especially when we go out of our way to avoid other people. Some of our research showed in other contexts that we avoid information from other people that can remind us of the fact that we are not having momentum toward our goal. And even though donors are very helpful . . . we may be fearful and want to avoid them at that stage, because we worry about reporting progress to them, or even just talking about the campaign in general as we're not feeling that internal drive. (Huang 2024)

So, when we are feeling self-doubt or insecure, we shy away from situations where we feel like someone might express disappointment in us, or even just remind us that we feel disappointed in ourselves or are doubting our capabilities. But even though it is scary to reach out amid our self-doubt or send another email about our campaign, Huang's research shows this is the most critical time to do so. The connection will help us overcome self-doubt, rejuvenate our motivation, and deepen relationships instead.

Developing deep connections takes time, energy, and personal investment. This isn't something you want to throw away. One other way to create additional motivation and accountability for retention and stewardship activities inside your organization is to start to track the behaviors and habits you want to be taking, instead of just looking at fundraising outcomes. The work of behavior scientist Dr. BJ Fogg, Founder and Director of the Stanford Behavior Design Lab, inspired my shift in focus toward recognizing fundraiser behaviors as the leading indicator, instead of focusing on the lagging indicator of fundraising outcomes. Here's a simple way you can start to embrace this shift in focus: brainstorm all of your behaviors that create engagement, community, and deepen connection. Start to track those behaviors personally and as a team, and make sure to celebrate them in the moment and reinforce those behaviors in weekly staff meetings, board meetings, and wherever else is appropriate. What you focus on and celebrate grows.

Staying focused on remaining connected with aligned partners creates more ease and potential for growth in organizations. Ideally, your reason for investing in retention and stewardship strategies is that it's the right thing to do for the health of the relationship you have with your donors. How do you think it feels when an organization spends time and energy encouraging a donor to make a gift and afterward offers only silence or a generic tax receipt? Can you imagine if you dropped off dinner at a friend's house and never heard anything? I'm not saying we need to put our donors on a pedestal above us or the communities we serve, but we should acknowledge them and their investment because that's how we behave in healthy relationships. If this isn't enough to incentivize stewardship, the business reason should seal the deal: it costs way more to acquire a new donor than to retain a donor (Association of Fundraising Professionals 2023).

Most of the time, we can't foster one-on-one relationships with every single donor. But if we are implementing an aligned strategy that focuses on authentic connection points, we can still build relationships through our marketing, bulk communications, and so on. This enables us to foster a deeper feeling of belonging and connection, and ultimately see better results.

Actions That Break Trust and Connection

We started Part 2 by talking about how Alignment Fundraising is rooted in our connection to ourselves through our consciousness of our thoughts, beliefs, feelings, and behavior. Not only does our initial energy level and stress affect our ability to connect with donors but also the management of our inner experience over time constantly influences trust, connection, and relationships.

When we're stressed, and revert back into transactional fundraising methods as a result, a whole host of challenges arise, many of which erode trust by leading us into relationship cycles where we are less transparent or authentic, and sometimes even disingenuous. Trust development experts Roy Lewicki and Chad Brinsfield (2017), as well as *Harvard Business Review* contributors Robert Galford and Anne Seibold Drapeau (2003), have identified a range of factors that show how transactional fundraising and misalignment break trust:

- **False feedback.** This is rooted in dishonesty, regardless of the intention. Perhaps you tell a funder that a truck would be the perfect donation because you don't want to offend them, but they later learn it wasn't the best use of their money.
- **Ignoring "elephants in the parlor."** As stated by Galford and Drapeau (2003), "Some situations are so painful or politically charged that it's easier to pretend that they don't exist." But avoiding uncomfortable conversations, or sending a bulk email that seems tone-deaf to the moment, could be interpreted as hiding information and can damage trust.
- **Early violations.** Trust can be especially fragile when it's first developing. If you make initial promises to a funder that you aren't able to keep, this can quickly undermine trust. Be honest about your capacity and what is and is not in alignment with your organization.
- **Behavioral disintegrity.** This occurs when someone feels you had poor judgment or made an incorrect decision. For example, when a fundraiser doesn't take a donor's no at face value and tries to override their no instead, we demonstrate that we don't respect the donor's boundaries and are creating a culture of pressure that undermines future engagement. We can't talk about wanting to set better boundaries for ourselves on the one hand and then not respect someone else's boundaries on the other.
- **Perceived intentionality.** If someone thinks you purposefully violated their trust, it can be particularly harmful to a relationship. This might happen when you set up a "listening" meeting and emphasize you just want to get to know the donor, but end up asking for a donation once you sit down at the table.

It's worth reiterating: attempting to present a perfectly curated version of ourselves or our organization is also a recipe for distrust. Our communication will give the impression of insincerity if we're simply telling the funder what we think they want to hear. Other people can tell when we're not being genuine and authentic. Perfectionism is a form of protection for ourselves; it doesn't build connected relationships.

When operating under chronic stress and burnout, it's nearly if not completely impossible to avoid all of the behaviors just mentioned, sabotaging our ability to build long-term, mutually beneficial relationships. Therefore, all of the strategies in this chapter that focus on strengthening alignment through connection require that we use the executive coaching strategies in Chapter 4 as we put them into practice.

You Won't Be for Everyone

By now, we understand that prioritizing alignment means focusing on the right funders. It means we will be in alignment with some funders and out of alignment with others—we will not be for everyone, and we shouldn't be. Sometimes, we'll see misalignment right away, but sometimes we won't see it until the relationship has progressed. It is possible to grow apart from a relationship that was once aligned. These shifts indicate that it's time to renegotiate the expectations of the relationship to realign or move on from the partnership.

Renegotiating is an important part of Alignment Fundraising. As you've been learning about yourself and new ways to fundraise in this book, you might have realized you hold a number of funder relationships that are not aligned. Before you give up on them, I encourage you to lean into the relationship and see if there is an opportunity for alignment. It's normal for discomfort to come up when renegotiating, and it might seem easier or more comfortable to move on, but like any real relationship, we want to give people the opportunity to come along with us.

I talked to Rachel D'Souza about this in relation to Community Centric Fundraising—a fundraising model grounded in equity and social justice by prioritizing the entire community over individual organizations—which is complementary to Alignment Fundraising (D'Souza 2024). When shifting to Alignment Fundraising practices, it's not necessary to wipe the slate clean. These methods give us the opportunity to share honestly with our funders, and invite them to interact in a new, more beneficial way with our community and organizational needs at the core.

"You would say to your partner, to a friend, to a family member, 'Hey, it's been like this for a while, and it's not really working for me. So, I think it's time to try something new.'" She explains that oftentimes in nonprofits we don't want to invest in that same type of planning or creating buy-in with constituents. But, as she explains, "When you are in a relationship with someone that is authentic, you bring them along" (D'Souza 2024).

D'Souza demonstrates how we can renegotiate these relationships so the donor feels informed instead of blindsided by change. "So, what does it look like to say, 'Hey, I know this is what our relationship has looked like for the last five years. And here's what our organization has been through. And now I want to open the door to having a different conversation with you'" (D'Souza 2024).

As you navigate donor relationships, bring awareness to the power dynamics at play and how they can affect your organization and funders. Although many fundraisers tend to believe we have no power, which escalates our discomfort to chronic stress, we actually have more influence than we think. This doesn't mean conversations will always be comfortable or without fear, but this is another place we can use the strategies in Chapter 4 to stay true to our values and in alignment. A great example is how we facilitate the overhead conversation rooted in these principles.

Discussing Overhead

We've talked about the scarcity mindset and limiting beliefs that relate to overhead, but how do we connect the inner belief work and alignment with funders to have a tactical conversation about something vulnerable like overhead instead of perpetuating the scarcity belief itself?

Assuming that we understand our influence in the overhead conversation, our inherent value and assets, and we aren't getting trapped in scarcity mindset, we're ready to confront the overhead conversations head on. Here are a few ways in which I've coached fundraisers to broach the subject while staying connected to ourselves, our mission, and our funders at the same time:

- "I understand that other nonprofits you support spend less on overhead. However, we are committed to fully supporting our staff with a living wage. We believe in living out our core values through not only the external services that we provide but also our internal culture and workplace environment."
- "I understand that other nonprofits you support spend less on overhead, but we believe that the 'overhead myth' is a really problematic narrative in our sector. Overhead is not inherently bad, and we are proud of the way we allocate our funds to maximize results."
- "We hear you when you say it's unnerving to see funding go to operations when you are feeling the stress and pressure of addressing x issue in our community. We love how passionate you are about x. That's why we'd love to take some time to walk through how investment in our operations results in x."
- "What I hear you saying is that the money we spend on operations doesn't feel like direct program impact. I would love the opportunity to explain to you how deeply they are connected and why it's so important for us to value the quality of our operations."

With all of this in mind, sometimes we can do everything possible on our end to build a healthy relationship where we believe alignment exists, and yet there is a growing disconnect or misalignment with the funder. When this happens, and we can't renegotiate our relationship, our ability to show up as our authentic selves decreases and the best course of action is to leave that relationship behind.

In the overhead conversation, that might sound like this: "It doesn't seem like we are finding common ground when it comes to the value of *x* spending. However, our position is non-negotiable and we will not devalue this work in order to receive funds. We would love to help you find an organization that is more aligned with your investment values."

Aside from overhead, there are many valuable reasons to move away from donors who aren't right for you. Our time is valuable, and we can't expect ourselves to chase misaligned partnerships or contort ourselves to the whims and desires of funders. When we accept that some people are not for us, we can move away from engaging in toxic relationships and start to find funders who truly value us and our organization.

The idea of being able to say goodbye to donors who aren't the right fit is empowering. It enables us to have clarity, focus, and fundraise in a way that feels good to everyone involved. As Seth Godin said, "As soon as you are willing to get rid of 10% of your donors, you will serve the other 90% dramatically better because it will force you to be clear about what's on offer" (Godin 2022). This is Alignment Fundraising.

Letting Go

Working for a nonprofit, we are asked to do so much "for the cause." We're treated as though we shouldn't need to make more money because of our passion-driven work—we're asked to work weekends, nights, bend over backward, and take on responsibilities well outside of our role. Beyond the fact that these expectations are harmful and inappropriate, we cannot ignore that everything about our work is made personal and often feels personal. And yet, when we get rejected by a funder, we are immediately told "don't take it personally." The double standard here is outrageous. Of course we take it personally. In addition to the fact that rejection understandably hurts our feelings, rejection feels even more personal when someone says no to being involved in something that is tied so closely to our identity. Acknowl-edging and validating our feelings doesn't mean the reason they didn't give *was* personal; it just enables us to move through our feelings related to the rejection.

After acknowledging and validating your feelings, it can be helpful to reframe the rejection toward a belief that there wasn't alignment instead of blaming yourself or believing you or your organization is unworthy. Additionally, I think it's important to acknowledge that the natural occurrence of rejection in fundrais-ing might require some of us to take space and time to process our feelings about rejection.

I spoke about this with Arosha Brouwer, cofounder and CEO at Quan, a platform to support sustainable workplace environments through science-based inquiry and behavioral insight:

> It's interesting that you mentioned that there's so much focus on skill development as the answer for the chronic issues fundraisers are having. It's a little bit like how everybody wants to talk about performance and how to increase performance. And everybody likes the analogy of athletes. Leaders talk about the performance of those athletes, but they don't talk about the fact that 10% is actually performance and 90% is recovery. And that's why the athlete can perform during the time that they need to because they're actually taking care of themselves for the remaining 90% of the time.
>
> And fundraising and sports are actually very similar: both are jobs with very clear targets.
>
> So, it is not about shaking [it] off and just game-timing and pushing through. Sometimes it's more about recognizing when things are not OK, so you can attend to that, so that you can rejuvenate so that you're in a good state to go back and do the performance. (Brouwer 2023)

Brouwer further acknowledged that nobody likes rejection; if all you're doing is trying to close the deal, and you don't actually process the rejection and figure out what you need in order to get back up and try again, you're going to deplete your resources (Brouwer 2023). If athletes' greatness is partially attributed to the ample rest they get, why do we think we can bounce from rejection to the next donor meeting without affecting our performance or energy? This expectation seems fundamentally unreasonable.

We have to give ourselves the time and space to process our emotions and deal with rejection instead of always expecting ourselves to jump right back in the game and move on to the next funder. We need to stop pushing ourselves to do more when what we actually need is to feel more.

When It All Aligns

Do you remember my donor Jeff from Chapter 2? He's the one I felt disappointed in when he gave the lowest sponsorship level for an event. He's the one I didn't value when I was programmed for a transactional way of fundraising. Well, our relationship didn't stop there. As I started to pull myself away from transactional fundraising methods, my relationship with Jeff changed.

I started to notice and appreciate how generous he was with his network. I noticed the areas of our program where he was the most excited, and asked for introductions and advocacy that would help strengthen the organization. In no time, Jeff was opening up doors left and right. When challenges arose, I would talk them through with Jeff, never downplaying or hiding what was happening inside the organization. I was vulnerable and honest, and in his acceptance of me, I started to see what connected donor relationships could feel like.

Then, our relationship was really tested. He invited me to lunch with funders of nonprofits committed to environmental sustainability. It was at a nice restaurant in North Beach, the Italian district of San Francisco. I was so nervous and hardly felt like I had the time to make the trek. I showed up scattered and stressed, straight from a garden workday. I knew I didn't want to miss a fundraising opportunity, so I brought some bars of chocolate our students sold. If I couldn't make a compelling case for the organization, at least I could give them chocolate bars with our mission statement on it. My resistance to fundraising was still there because, while I had an aligned relationship with Jeff, I didn't have all of the skills to manage my energy, the chatter in my head, or the scarcity mindset that was weighing me down in front of the new potential funders.

During lunch, I was fairly quiet and reserved, drowning in my own imposter syndrome. Jeff asked me to speak, and I gave a quick overview of the organization. I had to leave early, so I left the chocolate bars with everyone to share after lunch. When I got on the BART train to go home, I opened one of the chocolate bars for myself and was immediately horrified. Inside the chocolate bar, moths were covering the backside. Yes, moths, the bugs. I immediately began to panic, imagining all of the funders taking a bite of the chocolate only to discover they had just eaten a bug!

I had to get a message to all of them right away to tell them not to eat it, but I didn't have anyone's contact information other than Jeff. Besides the fact that I knew I definitely wasn't getting any funding from that group of funders, I was terrified to tell Jeff. He had trusted me with all of these relationships, he had taken a chance on me and I was scared he was going to be mortified and angry. I was sure I had ruined my relationship with him.

I sent him a text and an email immediately telling him what had happened in hopes of intercepting the situation before anyone opened the bars. I didn't hear back from him for hours, so I have no idea what happened at that table in North Beach, but the email I got back from him went something like this: "Mallory! Loved having you at lunch. Don't worry at all, some of my favorite sweaters have moth holes and I still love them:). See you soon?"

I remember the moment I read the email on my phone, standing in the middle of my bedroom. My whole body relaxed and I took a deep breath. I felt seen, appreciated, connected, and whole. I didn't need to be perfect for him to value me, my organization, or my work. Something inside of me clicked in that moment and I knew that this is what alignment feels like. This is what connected relationships feel like. Jeff passed away a few years ago, and I continue to tell this story because I am so grateful for what he taught me about what's possible when we fundraise in alignment.

Fundraising, nonprofit leadership, and changemaking is hard. Change is hard. Small steps and continuous improvement will help you and your nervous system start to build a new baseline. As you start to move toward fundraising with more alignment, it's normal to experience doubt. Doubt is part of the journey, and it can lead us to default to the old ways of doing things. I hope that in those moments you lean into the community that makes you feel the most aligned, or come back to this book and think about Jeff. We are not always going to get it right (although I really hope you don't have to deal with moth-eaten chocolate), but we can find partners who come along with us through all the ups and downs.

That is what Alignment Fundraising is all about.

Conclusion

Fundraising sits at the intersection of many contradictions. It can be both defeating and frustrating, but also some of the most rewarding and sacred work. It is about people and relationships, but it is also about resources and the movement of those resources. Fundraising is about solving inequities, but it often perpetuates them, too. So much of my day-to-day involves grappling with deep frustration at the broken system while providing specific resources to improve the lives of fundraisers working inside that same system.

Being a fundraiser means living in the gray, trying to find the balance and the nuance between what, at first glance, might feel diametrically opposed. I say this because, from my perspective, the sector is currently stuck in a trope of seeing everything in a binary way: givers or takers, donors or fundraisers. This creates a terrible narrative because no one is an ATM, and no one is a bottomless well of need. Because of power imbalances and toxic dynamics tied to money, we often forget that people are inherently generous, and almost everyone is a donor or connected to nonprofits through at least one degree of separation, if not directly. As Community-Centric Fundraising continues to remind us—the community benefits *most* when everyone both gives and receives. Everyone is human and deserves to be treated with the dignity and value that we inherently hold.

We all have a stake in the health of this sector.

Our sector relies on the movement of money, yet money also creates the dynamics that lead to the discomfort showing up in the brains and bodies of fundraisers, and often donors, too. I remember talking to a donor once who had just made a $3 million pledge to an organization. I was talking to her about the fundraising she was doing for another organization, and even though she knew how wonderful it felt to invest in something she believed in, she still had butterflies in her stomach thinking about inviting someone else to have the same experience. Our beliefs and the stigmas about money, value, self-worth, and asking for help run deep. No matter who you are, feelings of overwhelm, fear, and scarcity arise when we talk about money. It's normal. When I feel overwhelmed by the idea of asking for money, I try to remember who is on the other side of that invitation: another human being who desires the same things. And all humans desire the same things: connection and a sense of belonging. And that's exactly what this sector, and everyone in it, needs to thrive.

Throughout this book, we've heard from experts who have emphasized the importance of connection, alignment, and community. We've heard how those themes can enable us to reach our goals and help us have a more emotionally sustainable experience as we try to change the world for the better. Although each conversation is unique, the same themes emerge in nearly every one of my podcast episodes.

Connection is the cornerstone of nonprofit fundraising, yet we have not done nearly enough to enable fundraisers with the space, capacity, or support to connect with themselves, each other, or donors in real and sustained ways. Because our primary mode of connection is through our emotions, we have to create more space for fundraisers to acknowledge their emotions and address them in healthy and holistic ways. Our ability to do this requires a collective acknowledgment of fundraisers' current experiences.

For most of the fundraisers I talk to, all they truly want is to be able to fundraise in a way that feels good and authentic. In my work, I have found that what we need more than anything—more than tactics, tools, skill development, or even time management strategies—is connection. When we are connected and aligned, we find our ability to build real relationships with the people around us and make the changes we wish to see in our organizations, communities, and the world. This is true fundraiser enablement. As Dr. Carole Robin eloquently said, "People do business with people. They don't do business with ideas, machines, products, strategies, or money. So, unless you get the people part right, you will be limited in how successful you will be" (Robin 2023).

We have not been getting the people part right, especially within our organizations.

To fully embrace and enable the people behind the purpose, we need systemic changes that don't penalize risk, perpetuate a scarcity mindset, or continue to reinforce transactional fundraising practices. As we move away from these behaviors that have historically promoted stress and burnout, we must also equip fundraisers with the space and new tools to avoid the destructive slide into burnout and create sustainable and authentic relationships with funders and others in our field. That is the core of doing our work well and staying connected to it.

If we can get this right, we can reverse the trends the sector is currently facing: an overall decline in giving, a community of defeated fundraisers, and a society that profoundly needs both to be reversed. But flipping the trends in the sector is a collective responsibility. We need to remember we're all in this together. As we discussed, trust plays a key role in nonprofit support. Trust is built by individuals and organizations, but it also exists at the systems level. As I mentioned previously, the average donor supports five to seven organizations (Dietz and Keller 2016). This means we're ultimately stewarding each other's donors; our work is interconnected and interdependent, and we'll be more effective at building trust if we do it together with a collective vision. This is why we must come together with a unified mission to move more money into the nonprofit sector and to do this while keeping our people well.

In addition to trying to inspire collective ownership, my other goal in writing this book is to support those who suffer from fundraising discomfort and overwhelm. My hope is that the tools provided here help prevent your decline into chronic stress and burnout through the executive coaching and alignment frameworks. As I said previously, no amount of inner work can completely make up for a toxic environment. But it doesn't mean it doesn't help. For me, these tools were profound, but change did not happen overnight. Sometimes change initially activated my nervous system because it provoked feelings of uncertainty and fear of the unknown. In those moments, I turned to many of the same tools discussed in Chapter 4 to address my self-doubt and harness my energy. As you try out and adopt the strategies in this book, I hope you do so with self-compassion, grace, and the goal of one-degree shifts. A one-degree shift every day will ultimately change your entire orientation. That's what leads you to living and fundraising in alignment.

Alignment is your best tool for moving your mission forward. When we focus on alignment in our relationships, they feel good. It doesn't mean we don't experience discomfort or stress from time to time, but we feel a sense of clarity, calm, and emotional flexibility that enables us to avoid the typical challenges that lead to burnout. We can learn and practice tools together to help us stay connected and empower us to do what matters most: building magnetic relationships that change the world.

I believe this is possible because I believe in you.

So, I want to end this book with two questions:

- What will be possible when we improve the lives of fundraisers and reverse the trends in giving to the nonprofit sector?

- What will be possible when nonprofits become the remedy and community people are looking for to live more connected and meaningful lives?

I say "when" not "if" because I truly believe we can do this. I believe we can have sustainable careers rooted in belonging, connected relationships, and emotional wellness. More than anything, I believe in you, fundraisers. And I will be here with you, cheering you on and learning alongside you every step of the way.

Acknowledgments

Over the last few months, I kept getting alerts on my phone that my heart rate had risen above 120 beats per minute while I seemed to be inactive. It turns out that writing this book was hard. It took me 18 months to even agree to it, and another 4 months to actually start writing. It's funny that so much of this book is about self-doubt, overwhelm, and paralysis, but there I was in all of my own imposter syndrome and completely paralyzed. I always say that everything I talk about and teach in my work is a practice I use on a daily basis. It's true, and it's how I stay in action 98% of the time. But sometimes, for all of us, the paralysis runs deeper, and it takes longer to move through our resistance.

I was terrified to write this book for several reasons. First, I thought I was too early in this work to make my voice important enough for a book. After all, I only started my full practice in 2021. I had all the perfectionist narratives that said, "I will be ready when," but I acknowledged them for what they were and said yes anyway. I hope this inspires others to take the leap before you're ready, too. The second reason for my resistance is I know my research is incomplete. Every day, I am learning, growing, and doing new research on the *What the Fundraising* podcast. How could I publish something that I can't just delete a few days later if I change my mind? For someone who is constantly iterating on their work, this idea is agonizing.

But once again, I saw the thoughts and the beliefs for what they were, and said yes anyway. I was scared; I did it anyway, but I definitely didn't do it alone.

I'm a fundraiser at heart, so I have no shortage of genuine gratitude that I need to express.

First, the person who had to deal with my constant oscillation between excitement and panic as I took on this project is my husband, Ryan, without whom none of my work would be possible. Ryan supported me in getting certified as a coach and launching my business in the middle of COVID with no childcare and no financial backdrop, and he has believed in me and cheered me on even when I didn't think I could do it. During every tech meltdown, confusing legal issue, and contractor crisis, he steps up and steps in to help me in any way he can. There is no way I could have taken this on without knowing I had him behind me and beside me every step of the way. Ryan, I know how lucky I am—thank you for loving and supporting me through all of life's ups and downs.

I also could never have written this book without my best friend, Lindsey Shively. Linds is not only the smartest person I know (and I know a lot of smart people), but having been best friends for just shy of 25 years, she understands me better than anyone (sorry, Ryan). When I couldn't see the forest for the trees, she stepped in and guided me through. Linds, I wouldn't have made it through this without you. Through our broken noses, French class, bad trips, and a lifetime of our best and worst moments together, you make everything better while teaching me so much about sufficiency, connection, and wholeness. I cannot imagine life without you.

In addition to Lindsey's guidance, three people made this book considerably more readable than my ADHD brain would have on its own. Isabella Masucci, thank you for your help as a writing coach. Kayla Young, thank you for your unwavering research support. And Alexa Gorman, thank you for your editing, feedback, and support—I truly could not have done this without you.

There were many bumps along the way writing this book and the biggest one happened two months after I had a baby. Cameron Clark, you are what friend dreams are made of. Thank you for having my back and best interest in mind, and helping me navigate an unprecedented challenge. Kyle Endicott, your guidance and sound mind got me through some very stressful moments and this book exists today thanks to your support.

Many people—whether they know it or not—enabled me to write this book. Starting and running a business alone is scary, hard, and isolating—my community makes every day more manageable (and a heck of a lot more fun). From my text chain with Kishshana Palmer, Dana Snyder, and Becky Endicott to my weekly calls with Vik Harrison and A. J. Mizes when we were building our courses, to connecting at conferences and in my home with Donovan Taylor Hall, Floyd Jones, Jon McCoy, Lisa Tarshis, Michelle Shireen Muri, Natalie Monroe, and Rhea Wong—my friendships in this space have created synergy in my life that makes both my work and life more meaningful. When I look around and see my daughter making s'mores with a kit from Nathan Chappell, who is not only my partner with Fundraising.AI but was also the friend who gave me the final push to sign a publishing agreement, I know I have found my people and my purpose. And today, I am no longer alone in my business either. I am so grateful to Jess Spino and Jen Lau for their partnership in building my business and Fundraising. AI—your commitment to me, this sector, and improving the lives of fundraisers is not something I take lightly. Thank you for everything you do to keep me on track and on purpose.

My friends and colleagues in this space have pushed me to think bigger and more critically—whether they know it or not. In addition to those already mentioned and in this book, my research has been driven by the encouragement and support of April Walker, BJ Fogg, Dennis Boyle, Duke Stump, Jay Love, Jeff Vogel, Julie Confer, Justin McCord, Kelley Hecht, Libby DeLana, Lou Cove, Maggie Doyne,

Meena Das, Natalie Rekstad, Nejeed Kasam, Rachel D'Souza, Rebecca Blanck-Weiss, Seth Godin, Stephanie Weldy, Tim Lockie, Tim Sarrantonio, Whitney Clapper, and Woodrow Rosenbaum, and all of the guests who have joined me on *What the Fundraising* to push me and this conversation forward—I am so grateful to all of you.

I also need to thank the following companies for believing in me and my work, and for supporting the research I do on *What the Fundraising* through their sponsorship and content partnerships: Bloomerang, Constant Contact, Cosmic, DonorPerfect, Feathr, Givebutter, Instil, Keela, Kindsight, Learn Grant Writing, Nation-Builder, Neon One, Overflow, Pledge, and Stock Donator. None of the conversations quoted in this book would have been possible without you. Thank you for seeing the value in this body of work from the beginning. And tremendous thanks to Patagonia for their support in amplifying this work further.

Three friends and mentors of mine deserve special recognition as well. Thank you to Karen Mulvaney for teaching me so much about emotion, and what it looks like to let yourself be led by deep feelings. To Laura Talmus for showing me what graceful and bold nonprofit leadership looks like. You both saw something in me before I could see it myself, and I'm so grateful for your endless love and encouragement. To Steve Gomberg, thank you for helping me access my leadership potential, and for believing in me and supporting me through some epic nonprofit crises. You've all taught me a lot and stood by me when I felt alone.

To Anna Beuselinck, Madeline McNeely, Michelle Vos, and Ruthie Lindsey, each of you helped me find my way home to myself at some of the most critical moments in my life. Thank you for your guidance and love.

I agreed to write this book at possibly one of the hardest times of my life. I was pregnant with my second daughter, horribly sick for 24 weeks with morning sickness, followed by having a new baby. I am not quite sure what I was thinking when I agreed to do this, but I'm ever grateful for the Wiley team, particularly Brian Neill and

Gabriela Mancuso, for all of the guidance and support, especially in my postpartum daze and overwhelm.

I cannot write my thanks and gratitude without acknowledging the people who taught me about generosity in the first place—my parents and grandparents. I'm so grateful that I grew up understanding that my family had been beneficiaries of nonprofits when they first came to this country, and then watching them give back once they got on their own two feet. My Grandma Rose's life as a Holocaust survivor oriented me toward justice work from a young age and her legacy remains close to my heart as a North Star.

On my dad's side of the family, I was always surrounded by acts of generosity, too. I remember my dad telling a story about his parents' accountant who often told them they were "giving too much away" every year. They didn't care. My Grandma Marj and Grandpa Ed were constantly thinking about those around them and were examples of generosity.

But my parents taught me the most about generosity—from the way they gave to local organizations, attended fundraising events, and wove nonprofits into our lives in countless ways (not to mention all the years they donated to the nonprofits where I worked). My siblings and I grew up watching our parents show up for us and for our community. Mom and Dad, thank you for continuously showing me what generosity looks and feels like.

There are so many other people who supported me to make this (and all my work) possible, from my siblings, friends, and neighbors who brought meals while I edited and baby carried, to the endless number of consultants, companies, and thought leaders that supported my research on *What the Fundraising* and then sent baby gifts, meals, and cheered me on. I feel so connected and aligned with all of you. Whether it's through social media, emails, text messages, voice memos, or in-person hugs, you are always in my heart and on my mind. I cannot name everyone, the list is too long, but I want you to know that every word of encouragement is felt and appreciated. I see my work as the product of an interconnected network of learning, collaboration, and exploration. I am surrounded by the best people. From my community to content partners to Fundraising. AI sponsors—all of whom want to see this sector thrive—you give me hope.

Finally, to the fundraisers: none of this would mean anything if it weren't for you. In addition to the amazing fundraisers who shared case studies in this book—Ben Houghton, Heather Hooper, Hilary Wolkan, Liberty Franks, and Stacey Levy—thousands of you have let me into your lives and organizations over the years to hear the vulnerable stories of your discomfort, overwhelm, and burnout. I've been honored to sit with and support so many of you to fundamentally change the way you fundraise and then witness your success. You always had it inside of you. Every person who joins the Power Partners Formula™ and every message I get about a webinar, speaking engagement, or a *What the Fundraising* episode motivates me to do more and show up more for you and this sector. Thank you for letting me be a part of your journey and making it to the end of this very long book!

Many of you might have opened this book thinking that it's a book about fundraising. But it's actually a book about fundraisers. I see fundraisers as the linchpin for changing our sector, which is why their wellness and wholeness are so critical to all of our work. So now that we know this, what are we going to do about it?

References

Allen, Nneka, Pereira Camila Vital Nunes, and Nicole Salmon, eds. 2020. *Collecting courage: Joy, pain, freedom, love—Anti-Black racism in the charitable sector* (Toronto: Gail K. Picco).

Alshak, Mark N., and Joe M. Das. 2024. "Neuroanatomy, Sympathetic Nervous System." *StatPearls* (January 2024). https://pubmed.ncbi .nlm.nih.gov/31194352/.

Andersen, Martin M., Somogy Varga, and Anna P. Folker. 2022. "On the Definition of Stigma." *Journal of Evaluation in Clinical Practice* 28(5): 847–853. https://doi.org/10.1111/jep.13684.

Anderson, Cameron, and Jennifer L. Berdahl. 2002. "The Experience of Power: Examining the Effects of Power on Approach and Inhibition Tendencies." *Journal of Personality and Social Psychology* 83(6): 1362–1377. https://psycnet.apa.org/record/2002-08203-011.

Arnsberger, Paul, Melissa Ludlum, Margaret Riley, and Mark Stanton. 2008. "A History of the Tax-Exempt Sector: An SOI Perspective." *Statistics of Income Bulletin* (Winter): 105–135. https://www.irs.gov/ pub/irs-soi/tehistory.pdf.

Association of Fundraising Professionals. 2019. "Fundraisers Satisfied with Many Aspects of Their Job, but Half Likely to Leave Current Position in Two Years." *AFP Research & Reports*, August 6. https:// afpglobal.org/fundraisers-satisfied-many-aspects-their-job-half-likely-leave-current-position-two-years#:~:text=Eighty%2Dfour

%20percent%20feel%20tremendous,over%20the%20next%20 two%20years.

Association of Fundraising Professionals. 2023. "Donor Retention: How to Sustain Relationships Year After Year." *Guides and Resources*, July 6. https://afpglobal.org/donor-retention-how-sustain-relationships-year-after-year.

Barrett, Lisa Feldman. 2018. *How Emotions Are Made: The Secret Life of the Brain* (Boston: Mariner Books).

Barrett, Lisa Feldman. 2020. *Seven and a Half Lessons About the Brain* (New York: Houghton Mifflin Harcourt).

Barrett, Lisa Feldman. 2021a. "How Emotions Are Made and Why It Matters for Fundraisers." *What the Fundraising* podcast, August 24. https://malloryerickson.com/podcast/how-emotions-are-made-why-it-matters-for-fundraisers-with-dr-lisa-feldman-barrett/.

Barrett, Lisa Feldman. 2021b. "Your Brain Is Not What You Think It Is, with Lisa Feldman Barrett, PhD." *Speaking of Psychology* podcast, April 28. https://www.apa.org/news/podcasts/speaking-of-psychology/brain-myths.

Bergland, Christopher. 2015. "The Neuroscience of Trust." *Psychology Today*, August 12. https://www.psychologytoday.com/us/blog/the-athletes-way/201508/the-neuroscience-trust.

Bernstein, Peter, and Annalyn Swan. 2008. *All the Money in the World: How the Forbes 400 Make—and Spend—Their Fortunes* (New York: Random House).

Bhui, Kamaldeep, Sokratis Dinos, Magdalena Galant-Miecznikowska, Bertine de Jongh, and Stephen Stansfeld. 2016. "Perceptions of Work Stress Causes and Effective Interventions in Employees Working in Public, Private and Non-governmental Organisations: A Qualitative Study." *BJPsych Bulletin* 40(6): 318–325. https://www.ncbi.nlm.nih.gov/pmc/articles/PMC5353523/.

Bianchi, Renzo, Irvin Sam Schonfeld, and Eric Laurent. 2015. "Is it Time to Consider the 'Burnout Syndrome' a Distinct Illness?" *Frontiers in Public Health* 8(3): 158. https://www.ncbi.nlm.nih.gov/pmc/articles/PMC4459038/.

Birrell, Jane, Kevin Meares, Andrew Wilkinson, and Mark Freeston. 2011. "Toward a Definition of Intolerance of Uncertainty: A Review of Factor Analytical Studies of the Intolerance of Uncertainty Scale." *Clinical Psychology Review* 31(7): 1198–1208. https://doi.org/10.1016/j.cpr.2011.07.009.

Bohns, Vanessa. 2021. *You Have More Influence Than You Think: How We Underestimate Our Power of Persuasion, and Why It Matters* (New York: W. W. Norton & Company).

Bohns, Vanessa. 2022. "You Have More Influence Than You Think (for Fundraisers and Funders) with Vanessa Bohns." *What the Fundraising* podcast, January 18. https://malloryerickson.com/podcast/episode-26-you-have-more-influence-than-you-think-fundraiser-addition-with-vanessa-bohns/.

Bradford, David, and Carole Robin. 2021. *Connect: Building Exceptional Relationships with Family, Friends, and Colleagues* (New York: Crown Currency).

Britton-Purdy, Jedediah, Amy Kapczynski, and David Singh Grewal. 2021. "How Law Made Neoliberalism." *Boston Review*, February 22. https://www.bostonreview.net/articles/how-law-made-neoliberalism/.

Brouwer, Arosha. 2023. "How a Metrics-Based Approach to Well-Being Boosts Creativity and Outcomes with Arosha Brouwer." *What the Fundraising* podcast, January 3. https://malloryerickson.com/podcast/episode-98-how-a-metrics-based-approach-to-well-being-boosts-creativity-and-outcomes-with-arosha-brouwer/.

Brown, Adrienne Maree. 2017. *Emergent strategy: Shaping change, changing worlds* (Chico, CA: AK Press).

Busch, Christian. 2020. *The Serendipity Mindset: The Art and Science of Creating Good Luck* (New York: Riverhead Books).

Busch, Christian. 2023. "Cultivating the Unexpected: About Daring to Embrace the Art & Science of Serendipity with Dr. Christian Busch." *What the Fundraising* podcast, January 10. https://malloryerickson.com/podcast/episode-99-cultivating-the-unexpected-about-daring-to-embrace-the-art-science-of-serendipity-with-dr-christian-busch/.

Cannon, W. B. 1915. *Bodily Changes in Pain, Hunger, Fear and Rage: An Account of Recent Researches into the Function of Emotional Excitement* (New York: D. Appleton & Company). https://doi.org/10.1037/10013-000.

Capital Group. 2018. "Wisdom of Experience." https://www.capital group.com/content/dam/cgc/shared-content/documents/reports/MFGEWP-062-1218O.pdf.

Carnegie, Andrew. 1989. "The Gospel of Wealth." *North American Review* 148(391): 653–664. https://www.jstor.org/stable/25101798?seq=2.

Chavis, David M., and Kien Lee. 2015. "What Is Community Anyway?" *Stanford Social Innovation Review*, May 12. https://ssir.org/articles/entry/what_is_community_anyway.

Cherry, Christal M. n.d. "Broken Crayons: What Happens When Non-profit Leadership Fails Fundraisers of Color." *Collecting Courage: Joy, Pain, Freedom, Love—Anti-Black Racism in the Charitable Sector.* Accessed February 29, 2024. https://www.collectingcourage.org/broken-crayons.

Chirumbolo, Antonio, Antonio Callea, and Flavio Urbini. 2022. "Living in Liquid Times: The Relationships Among Job Insecurity, Life Uncertainty, and Psychological Well-Being." *International Journal of Environmental Research and Public Health* 19(22): 15255. https://doi.org/10.3390/ijerph192215225.

Chu, Brianna, Komal Marwaha, Terrence Sanvictores, and Derek Ayers. 2022. "Physiology, Stress Reaction." *StatPearls.* https://www.ncbi.nlm.nih.gov/books/NBK541120/.

Clay, Rebecca A. 2022. "Are You Experiencing Compassion Fatigue?" *American Psychological Association*, July 11. https://www.apa.org/topics/covid-19/compassion-fatigue.

Cleveland Clinic. n.d. "Parasympathetic Nervous System (PSNS)." *Body Systems & Organs.* Accessed March 3, 2024. https://my.cleve landclinic.org/health/body/23266-parasympathetic-nervous-system-psns.

Cohen, Geoffrey L. 2022. "How the Need to Belong Drives Human Behavior." *Speaking of Psychology* podcast, September 14. https://www.apa.org/news/podcasts/speaking-of-psychology/human

-behavior#:~:text=really%20belong%20there.-,The%20desire%20
to%20belong%20is%20a%20fundamental%20part%20of%20
human,can%20have%20far%2Dreaching%20effects.

Cohen, Geoffrey L. 2023. "We Belong Together: How Communication
Fuels Connection and Community." *Think Fast, Talk Smart: Communication Techniques* podcast, August 8. https://www.gsb.stanford
.edu/insights/we-belong-together-how-communication-fuels-
connection-community.

Crimmins, Brian, Nathan Chappell, and Michael Ashley. 2022. *The
Generosity Crisis: The Case for Radical Connection to Solve Humanity's
Greatest Challenges* (Hoboken, NJ: John Wiley & Sons).

Curti, Merle, Judith Green, and Roderick Nash. 1963. "Anatomy of
Giving: Millionaires in the Late 19th Century." *American Quarterly*
15(3): 416–435. https://doi.org/10.2307/2711372.

Dana, Deb. 2018. *The Polyvagal Theory in Therapy: Engaging the Rhythm
of Regulation* (New York: W. W. Norton & Company).

Daniel, Janay, Judy Levine, David McGoy, Cynthia Reddick, and Hera
Syed. 2019. "Money, Power, and Race: The Lived Experiences of
Fundraisers of Color." Cause Effective. https://www.causeeffective
.org/preparing-the-next-generation/money-power-and-race.html.

Dietz, Rich, and Brandy Keller. 2016. *Donor Loyalty Study: A Deep
Dive into Donor Behaviors and Attitudes.* Abila. https://www.thenonpro
fittimes.com/wp-content/uploads/2016/04/Donor-Loyalty-
Study.pdf

Dorsey, Cheryl, Peter Kim, Cora Daniels, Lyell Sakaue, and Britt
Savage. 2020. "Overcoming Racial Bias in Philanthropic Funding."
Stanford Social Innovation Review, May 4. https://ssir.org/articles/
entry/overcoming_the_racial_bias_in_philanthropic_funding#.

D'Souza, Rachel. 2024. "Building Inclusive Fundraising Communities in a Diverse World with Rachel D'Souza." *What the Fundraising* podcast, April 9.

Dugas, Michel J., Patrick Gosselin, and Robert Ladouceur. 2001. "Intolerance of Uncertainty and Worry: Investigating the Specificity in a
Nonclinical Sample." *Cognitive Therapy and Research* 25 (October):
551–558. https://doi.org/10.1023/A:1005553414688.

Echoing Green. 2020. "Bridging Economic Opportunity Through OpenData."https://echoinggreen.org/wp-content/uploads/2020/09/Citi_Echoing-Green_Report_Bridging-Economic-Opportunity-Through-Open-Data.pdf.

Edelman Trust Barometer. 2023. *2023 Edelman Trust Barometer: Navigating a Polarized World.* https://www.edelman.com/trust/2023/trust-barometer.

Edworthy, Kathryn, Adrian Sargeant, and Jen Shang. 2022. *Relationship Fundraising 3.0: A Review, Assessment & Experimental Results.* Institute for Sustainable Philanthropy. https://www.philanthropy-institute.org.uk/relationship-fundraising-3.

Eskin, Jim. 2021. "Priority: Retain Your Fundraising Staff." Candid, March 11. https://blog.candid.org/post/priority-retaining-your-fundraising-staff/.

Faulk, Lewis, Mirae Kim, Teresa Derrick-Mills, Elizabeth T. Boris, Laura Tomasko, Nora Hakizimana, Tianyu Chen, Minjung Kim, and Layla Nath. 2021. *Nonprofit Trends and Impacts 2021.* Urban Institute, October 7. https://www.urban.org/research/publication/nonprofit-trends-and-impacts-2021.

Frank, Britt. 2022a. *The Science of Stuck: Breaking Through Inertia to Find Your Path Forward* (New York: TarcherPerigee).

Frank, Britt. 2022b. "The Science of Stuck & How to Move Forward in Your Fundraising with Britt Frank." *What the Fundraising* podcast, October 18. https://malloryerickson.com/podcast/episode-79-the-science-of-stuck-how-to-move-forward-in-your-fundraising-with-britt-frank/.

Frei, Frances X., and Anne Morriss. 2022. "Begin with Trust." *Harvard Business Review* (May–June). https://hbr.org/2020/05/begin-with-trust.

Fundraising Effectiveness Project. 2023. *Quarterly Fundraising Report: Q3 2023.* https://data.givingtuesday.org/fep-report/.

Galford, Robert M., and Anne Seibold Drapeau. 2003. "The Enemies of Trust." *Harvard Business Review* (February). https://hbr.org/2003/02/the-enemies-of-trust.

Gamboa, Glenn. 2023. "Charitable Giving in 2022 Drops for Only the Fourth Time in 40 Years: Giving USA Report." Associated Press, June 20. https://apnews.com/article/charitable-giving-decline-givingusa-report-becaca47cae4bc4f55063cc9f1c5865a.

Gandhi, Lakshmi. 2021. "The Transcontinental Railroad's Dark Costs: Exploited Labor, Stolen Lands." *History*, October 8. https://www.history.com/news/transcontinental-railroad-workers-impact.

The George Peabody Library. n.d. "History." Accessed February 29, 2024. https://web.archive.org/web/20100604172628/http://www.peabodyevents.library.jhu.edu/history.html.

Gino, Francesca. 2018. "The Business Case for Curiosity." *Harvard Business Review.* (September–October). https://hbr.org/2018/09/the-business-case-for-curiosity#the-business-case-for-curiosity.

Giving USA. 2017. "Giving to Religion." https://givingusa.org/just-released-giving-usa-special-report-on-giving-to-religion/.

Godin, Seth. 2022. "Effective Fundraising and Power Partner Principles with Seth Godin." *What the Fundraising* podcast, August 30. https://malloryerickson.com/podcast/episode-68-effective-fundraising-and-power-partner-principles-with-seth-godin/.

Gregory, Ann Goggins, and Don Howard. 2009. "The Nonprofit Starvation Cycle." *Stanford Social Innovation Review* 7(4): 49–53. https://doi.org/10.48558/6K3V-0Q70.

Hagenbaugh, Barbara. 2008. "Uncertainty Is the Enemy of Philanthropy." *USA Today*, October 7. https://usatoday30.usatoday.com/news/nation/charity/2008-10-07-charity-economy_N.htm.

Hager, Mark A., Thomas Pollak, Kennard Wing, and Patrick M. Rooney. 2004. "Getting What We Pay For: Low Overhead Limits Nonprofit Effectiveness." *Nonprofit Overhead Cost Project* 3 (August): 1–4. https://archives.iupui.edu/server/api/core/bitstreams/09f95b36-7e63-4004-b765-8c75ee0a358e/content.

Haynes, Emily, and Rashida Childress. 2022. "Desperately Seeking Fundraisers." *The Chronicle of Philanthropy*, November 1. https://www.philanthropy.com/article/desperately-seeking-fundraisers?sra=true&cid=gen_sign_in.

Huang, Szu-chi. 2024. "Motivation Dynamics in Successful Fund-raising Campaigns with Szu-chi Huang." *What the Fundraising* podcast, March 19.

INCITE!, ed. 2017. *The revolution will not be funded: Beyond the non-profit industrial complex* (Durham, NC: Duke University Press).

InDEEP Initiative. n.d. "Insights from the Field to Close the $2.7 Billion Funding Gap Between White-Led and BIPOC-Led Environmental and Conservation Organizations." Accessed February 29, 2024. https://static1.squarespace.com/static/582a3bdf6a4963a0eccfee40/t/6138e1f426fa8a281706815c/1631117813116/InDEEP+CTG+ExecSummary+v2.pdf.

Independent Sector. 2021. "Trust in Civil Society: Understanding the Factors Driving Trust in Nonprofits and Philanthropy." https://independentsector.org/wp-content/uploads/2022/07/trust-report-2021-8421.pdf

Indiana University Lilly Family School of Philanthropy. 2023. "New Report Examines Differences in Charitable Giving Patterns, Practices Among Communities of Color." *Lilly Family School of Philanthropy News*, November 14. https://philanthropy.iupui.edu/news-events/news/_news/2023/charitable-giving-patterns.html.

Indiana University Lilly Family School of Philanthropy. 2024. "The Giving Environment: Understanding Pre-Pandemic Trends in Charitable Giving." A report by the Indiana University Lilly Family School of Philanthropy. (2021). Accessed March 2, 2024. https://scholarworks.iupui.edu/server/api/core/bitstreams/f5f188c8-285e-4ddd-ab10-6da930d82c6f/content.

Institute for Quality and Efficiency in Healthcare. 2016. "How Does the Nervous System Work?" Informedhealth.org, August 19. https://www.ncbi.nlm.nih.gov/books/NBK279390/.

iPEC. n.d. "The Energy Leadership® Index Assessment." Accessed March 3, 2024. https://www.energyleadership.com/assessment.

Jones, Floyd. 2024. "Finding Belonging: Building Thriving Communities with Floyd Jones." *What the Fundraising* podcast, February 27. https://malloryerickson.com/podcast/172-finding-belonging-building-thriving-communities-with-floyd-jones/.

Jones, Jeffrey M. 2021. "U.S. Church Membership Falls Below Majority for First Time." Gallup, March 29, 2021. https://news .gallup.com/poll/341963/church-membership-falls-below-majority-first-time.aspx.

Joslyn, Heather. 2019. "Why Turnover Keeps Turning." *The Chronicle of Philanthropy*, August 4. https://sh.philanthropy.com/.

Kanter, Beth, and Aliza Sherman. 2016. *The Happy, Healthy Nonprofit: Strategies for Impact without Burnout* (Hoboken, NJ: John Wiley & Sons).

Kerszenbaum, Livi. 2023. "Volunteering: A Powerful Employee Engagement Strategy for Corporate Social Responsibility (CSR)." *Orange County United Way*, March 17. https://www.unitedwayoc .org/blog/volunteering-a-powerful-employee-engagement-strategy-for-corporate-social-responsibility-csr/.

Key, Kimberly. 2015. "The Dark Side of Deadlines." *Psychology Today*, June 15. https://www.psychologytoday.com/us/blog/ counseling-keys/201506/the-dark-side-of-deadlines.

Kross, Ethan. 2021a. *Chatter: The Voice in Our Head, Why It Matters, and How to Harness It* (New York: Crown).

Kross, Ethan. 2021b. "Harnessing Your Inner Voice for Fundraising Success with Dr. Ethan Kross." *What the Fundraising* podcast, July 19. https://malloryerickson.com/podcast/episode-1-harnessing-your-inner-voice-for-fundraising-success-with-dr-ethan-kross/.

Lewicki, Roy J., and Chad Brinsfield. 2017. "Trust Repair." *Annual Review of Organizational Psychology and Organizational Behavior* 4 (March): 287–313. https://psycnet.apa.org/doi/10.1146/annurev-orgpsych-032516-113147

Longa, Letizia Della, Irene Valori, and Teresa Farroni. 2021. "Interpersonal Affective Touch in a Virtual World: Feeling the Social Presence of Others to Overcome Loneliness." *Frontiers in Psychology* 12 (2021): 795283. https://doi.org/10.3389/fpsyg.2021.795283.

McNichols, Nicole K. 2021. "How Burnout Can Affect Your Relationship." *Psychology Today*, December 8. https://www .psychologytoday.com/us/blog/everyone-on-top/202112/ how-burnout-can-affect-your-relationship.

Morning Consult. 2022. "Most Trusted Brands 2022." https://morn ingconsult.com/most-trusted-brands-2022/.

Muri, Michelle Shireen. 2020. "The Power of a Fundraiser: Why You Are the Key to Systems Change." Community-Centric Fund- raising, July 12. https://communitycentricfundraising.org/2020/ 07/12/the-power-of-a-fundraiser-why-you-are-the-key-to- systems-change/.

Muri, Michelle Shireen. 2023. "Redefining Fundraising Through a Community-Centric Approach with Michelle Shireen Muri." *What the Fundraising* podcast, June 6. https://malloryerickson .com/podcast/episode-132-redefining-fundraising-through-a- community-centric-approach-with-michelle-shireen-muri/.

National Council of Nonprofits. "2023 Nonprofit Workforce Survey Results: Communities Suffer as the Nonprofit Workforce Short- age Crisis Continues." https://www.councilofnonprofits.org/files/ media/documents/2023/2023-nonprofit-workforce-survey- results.pdf.

NPOInfo. 2021. "Understand Your Data | Charitable Giving Statis- tics for 2022." *Data Statistics, Top Articles*, December 13. https:// npoinfo.com/charitable-giving-statistics/.

Office of the U.S. Surgeon General. 2023." Our Epidemic of Loneliness and Isolation: The U.S. Surgeon General's Advisory on the Heal- ing Effects of Social Connection and Community." https://www .hhs.gov/sites/default/files/surgeon-general-social-connection- advisory.pdf.

Orvell, Ariana, Brian D. Vickers, Brittany Drake, Phillippe Verduyn, Ozlem Ayduk, Jason Moser, John Jonides, and Ethan Kross. 2021. "Does Distanced Self-Talk Facilitate Emotional Regulation Across a Range of Emotionally Intense Experiences?" *Clinical Psychological Science* 9(1): 68–78. https://doi.org/10.1177/216770262095153.

Passaler, Linnea. 2023. "Fundraiser Wellness and Healing Your Nerv- ous System with Dr. Linnea Passaler." *What the Fundraising* podcast, April 18. https://malloryerickson.com/podcast/episode-

120-fundraiser-wellness-amp-healing-your-nervous-system-with-dr-linnea-passaler/.

Perry, Mark J. 2006. "The Fixed Pie Fallacy." AEIdeas, December 23. https://www.aei.org/carpe-diem/the-fixed-pie-fallacy/.

Pew Research Center. 2023. "Public Trust in Government: 1958–2023." September 19. https://www.pewresearch.org/politics/2023/09/19/public-trust-in-government-1958-2023/.

Ramchandani, Rinku. 2023. "The Importance of Donor Engagement: How Nonprofits Can Build Meaningful Relationships." Donor Participation Project, December 22. https://joindpp.org/the-importance-of-donor-engagement-how-nonprofits-can-build-meaningful-relationships/.

RKD Group. n.d. "Solid Gold: The Nonprofit Marketer's Guide to Trust." Accessed March 3, 2024. https://info.rkdgroup.com/donor-trust.

Robin, Carole. 2023. "Real Relationships: The Truth About Growing Connection & The Skills to Do It With Carole Robin." *What the Fundraising* podcast, March 7. https://www.youtube.com/watch?v=aQ-apXeiVJ4.

Roelofs, Karin. 2017. "Freeze for Action: Neurobiological Mechanisms in Animal and Human Freezing." *Philosophical Transactions B* 372(1718): 20160206. https://doi.org/10.1098/rstb.2016.0206.

Rosenbaum, Woodrow. 2022. "Mobilize Your Mission: Data-Driven Decision Making in a Recession with Woodrow Rosenbaum." *What the Fundraising* podcast, September 20. https://malloryerickson.com/podcast/episode-71-mobilize-your-mission-data-driven-decision-making-in-a-recession-with-woodrow-rosenbaum/.

Rosenbaum, Woodrow. 2024. "Decoding Generosity: Trends, Challenges, and Solutions in Nonprofit Giving with Woodrow Rosenbaum." *What the Fundraising*, podcast, April 16.

Russell Sage Foundation. n.d. "History of the Russell Sage Foundation." Accessed February 29, 2024. https://www.russellsage.org/about/history/.

Safronova, Valeriya. 2021. "How Women Are Changing the Philanthropy Game." *New York Times*, January 30. https://www.nytimes.com/2021/01/30/style/mackenzie-scott-prisclila-chan-zuckerberg-melinda-gates-philanthropy.html.

Sage, M. Olivia. 1905. "Opportunities and Responsibilities of Leisured Women." *The North American Review* 181(588): 712–721. http://www.jstor.org/stable/25105484.

Salamon, Lester M. 2018. *Nonprofits: America's Third Largest Workforce*. Johns Hopkins Nonprofit Data Project. http://ccss.jhu.edu/wp-content/uploads/downloads/2018/04/NED-46_National-2015_4.2018.pdf.

Sarno, John E. 1991. *Healing Back Pain: The Mind-Body Connection* (New York: Warner Books).

Schlund, Rachel, Roseanna Sommers, and Vanessa K. Bohns. 2024. "Giving People the Words to Say No Leads Them to Feel Freer to Say Yes." *Scientific Reports* 14(576). https://doi.org/10.1038/s41598-023-50532-3.

Schneider, Bruce D. 2022a. "The Energy Leadership® Index Assessment." iPEC Energy Leadership, https://www.energyleadership.com/assessment.

Schneider, Bruce D. 2022b. *Energy Leadership: The 7 Level Framework for Mastery in Life and Business*, 2nd ed. (Hoboken, NJ: John Wiley & Sons).

Seelig, Tina. 2009a. "The $5 Challenge." *Psychology Today*, August 5. https://www.psychologytoday.com/us/blog/creativityrulz/200908/the-5-challenge.

Seelig, Tina. 2009b. *What I Wish I Knew When I Was 20: A Crash Course on Making Your Place in the World* (New York: HarperCollins Publishers).

Shea, Christopher. 2016. "State of the Work: Stories from the Movement to Advance Diversity, Equity, and Inclusion." D5. https://www.d5coalition.org/wp-content/uploads/2016/04/D5-SOTW-2016-Final-web-pages.pdf.

Sinclair, Matt. 2023. "Nonprofits, Foundations Adjust to the Postpandemic Era." *Philanthropy News Digest*, March 30. https://

philanthropynewsdigest.org/news/nonprofits-foundations-adjust-to-the-post-pandemic-era.

Smith, Dana G. 2022. "How to Save Yourself from 'Task Paralysis.'" *New York Times*, December 12. https://www.nytimes.com/2022/12/12/well/mind/task-paralysis.html.

Srivastava, Sanjay, Maya Tamir, Kelly M. McGonigal, Oliver P. John, and James J. Gross. 2014. "The Social Costs of Emotional Suppression: A Prospective Study of the Transition to College." *Journal of Personality and Social Psychology* 96(4): 883–897. https://psycnet.apa.org/doi/10.1037/a0014755.

Steuerle, C. Eugene, and Benjamin Soskis. 2020. "Taxes and Foundations: A 50th Anniversary Overview." Tax Policy Center, February 8. https://www.urban.org/sites/default/files/publication/103608/taxes-and-foundations-a-50th-anniversary-overview_3.pdf.

Stump, Duke. 2021. "Reimagining Business and Partnerships for Good with Duke Stump." *What the Fundraising* podcast, August 31. https://malloryerickson.com/podcast/episode-8-reimagining-business-and-partnerships-for-good-with-duke-stump/.

Trusted Advisor Associates. 2020. "Understanding the Trust Equation," March 31. https://trustedadvisor.com/why-trust-matters/understanding-trust/understanding-the-trust-equation.

Twist, Lynne. 2017. *The Soul of Money: Reclaiming the Wealth of Our Inner Resources* (New York: W. W. Norton & Company).

Twist, Lynne. 2022. "How to Live a Committed Life & Raise Money from the Heart with Lynne Twist." *What the Fundraising* podcast, December 6. https://malloryerickson.com/podcast/episode-91-how-to-live-a-committed-life-raise-money-from-the-heart-with-lynne-twistepisode-91-how-to-live-a-committed-life-raise-money-from-the-heart-with-lynne-twist/.

Twist, Lynne, and Mary Earle Chase. 2023. *Living a committed life: Finding freedom and fulfillment in a purpose larger than yourself* (Oakland, CA: Berrett-Koehler).

Villanueva, Edgar. 2021. *Decolonizing Wealth: Indigenous Wisdom to Heal Divides and Restore Balance* (New York: Penguin Random House).

Yale University Medicine. n.d. "Chronic Stress." *Fact Sheets.* Accessed March 3, 2024. https://www.yalemedicine.org/conditions/stress-disorder#:~:text=%E2%80%A2A%20consistent%20sense%20of,weakness%2C%20less%20socialization%2C%20unfocused%20thinking.

Yu, Daniela, and Amy Adkins. 2016. "Charitable Giving: Donors Focus on One or Two Organizations." Gallup, June 14. https://news.gallup.com/businessjournal/192689/charitable-giving-donors-focus-one-two-organizations.aspx.

Weir, Kirsten. 2012. "The Pain of Social Rejection." *Monitor on Psychology* 43(4): 50. https://www.apa.org/monitor/2012/04/rejection.

Wilkins, Consuelo H. 2018. "Effective Engagement Requires Trust and Being Trustworthy." *Medical Care* 56 (October). https://doi.org/10.1097/MLR.0000000000000953.

Wiseman, Richard. 2003. *The Luck Factor: Changing Your Luck, Changing Your Life; The Four Essential Principles* (New York: Hyperion).

Zak, Paul J. 2017a. "The Neuroscience of Trust." *Harvard Business Review* (January–February). https://hbr.org/2017/01/the-neuroscience-of-trust.

Zak, Paul J. 2017b. *Trust Factor: The Science of Creating High-Performance Companies* (New York: AMACOM).

Zollo, Maurizio. 2021. "The Future of Cross-Sector Partnerships and the Key Roles for Nonprofits with Maurizio Zollo." *What the Fundraising* podcast, October 26. https://malloryerickson.com/podcast/the-future-of-cross-sector-partnerships-and-the-key-roles-for-nonprofits-with-maurizio-zollo/.

About the Author

Mallory Erickson is an executive coach and fundraising consultant who supports nonprofit leaders in fundamentally changing how they lead and fundraise. As the visionary behind the Power Partners Formula™ and the creator of the Alignment Fundraising methodology, Mallory has redefined how organizations engage with funders, moving away from a tunnel-visioned pursuit of money toward building authentic and impactful partnerships.

Combining her expertise in executive coaching with the science of behavior change and design thinking, Mallory has trained more than 60,000 fundraisers using elements of her unique, win-win framework. Each of her speaking engagements explores the intricacies of nonprofit fundraising, its intersection with behavioral science and psychology, and the cultivation of aligned partnerships. She demonstrates her dedication to altering the conventional fundraising narrative each time she steps on stage, urging us all to focus on the fundraiser rather than the fundraising.

Mallory's North Star is to improve the lives of fundraisers through holistic support. Since 2021, her contributions have garnered widespread recognition, establishing her as a leading voice in the field. Her commitment to meeting fundraisers at the intersection of overwhelm and enablement led to her involvement in launching Fundraising. AI and hosting the first Fundraising.AI Global Summit, which helps fundraisers use artificial intelligence responsibly and beneficially.

Mallory's efforts do more than just increase financial support; they inspire a collective shift toward making fundraising more approachable, human, and rooted in our connection to one another.

When she isn't discussing fundraising, Mallory enjoys time with her husband, Ryan, and her two daughters, Emmie and Ila, in Berkeley, California. She loves spending time outdoors, particularly in the redwoods, and always finds time for long walks and the people she loves.

Whether you are looking to hire Mallory to speak at your next event or are a fundraiser wanting to raise more from the right funders without hounding people for money, you can learn more about Mallory's work and current offerings at malloryerickson.com.

Index